Explore Macau

Explore Macau

A WALKING GUIDE AND HISTORY

Todd Crowell

BLACKSMITH BOOKS

Explore Macau

ISBN 978-988-19002-2-7

Published by Blacksmith Books
5th Floor, 24 Hollywood Road, Central, Hong Kong
Tel: (+852) 2877 7899
www.blacksmithbooks.com

Copyright © 2011 Todd Crowell

Maps by Katy Hung

CONTENTS

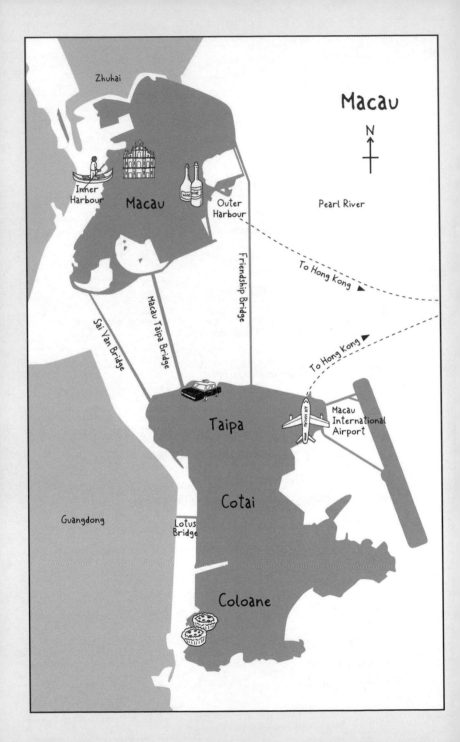

Introduction

Macau Overview

The origins of Macau are obscure. No treaty giving Macau to Portugal in perpetuity existed until the city was more than 300 years old. A strong tradition holds that local Chinese authorities in Guangdong province gave the Portuguese use of the obscure peninsula at the western entrance to the Pearl River Delta out of gratitude for their help in suppressing pirates. Conceivably, a document of some kind once existed, but may have been lost in transit to safety in the archives of Lisbon in a galleon, sunk in a storm or sea battle as many ships were in the early days of European exploration. Still, it is generally accepted that Portuguese began settling permanently on this spot around the year 1557. At that time, only three Chinese fishing villages dotted the small peninsula, along with a few temples or shrines, including the A-Ma Temple at the tip, which gives Macau its name (from *A Ma Gao*, or the Bay of A-Ma.) It has other names. To the Cantonese majority it is 澳門, *Ou-Mun*. To the mandarins in Beijing it is 澳门, *Aomen*. And since 1586 it has been officially styled *The City in the Name of God in China*.

The town grew quickly into the premier European outpost on the China coast. The Portuguese needed it as a way station in the chain of settlements stretching from Goa and Malacca supporting trade with Japan, which Lisbon held, for a time, as a monopoly. Canton (now more commonly called by its proper name Guangzhou) in China was closed to Europeans, so these imports moved through Macau. Then the Dutch captured Malacca (in modern Malaysia). Japan fell under the sway of the new Tokugawa ruler, who suppressed Christianity and closed Japan to all foreign intercourse except the Dutch, who were limited to a small island off Nagasaki. The Portuguese and Spanish monarchies broke their temporary union, which ended trade with Manila in the Philippines. Later, the British won and established a bigger and more robust trading post at Hong Kong. Macau went slowly but graciously to seed. Yet it has endured, its very seediness – expressed in crumbling old buildings, narrow streets or even in the modern gaudiness of its gambling emporiums – creating an ambience that makes it distinct from any other city in Asia.

The Chinese mainly looked on Macau as a kind of early treaty port, such as would later come to dot the rest of the coast. To the 16th-century Chinese who knew of them, Europeans' customs and manners seemed so strange that it was only natural that such a people needed to be segregated in their own small community where they could live and govern themselves without bothering the local population. In its earliest days, no Chinese were supposed to live permanently inside the enclave. They came to sell wares or labor by day but left by the barrier gate at night.

The Macanese governed themselves through their own Senate but paid a kind of rent to the adjacent Chinese district. In time, a network of fortifications was constructed across the middle of the peninsula and at other strategic points, but they were not intended to defend the tiny community from the Chinese. They were aimed at other Europeans. Indeed, in 1622 the Dutch did land at Macau but were repelled when a fortuitous cannon shot from the Monte Fort hit the invaders' ammunition train. The date, June 24, which happens to coincide with the saint day of the Portuguese patron St. John the Baptist, was celebrated as a holiday in the community until after the handover to Chinese sovereignty.

Sovereignty never became much of a concern until the 19th century, when it came to seem natural, to Europeans at least, that much of Asia would be colonized. Suddenly treaties and territorial rights took on new importance. The Portuguese observed how the British had rudely detached nearby Hong Kong Island from the Qing Dynasty in perpetuity after the Opium War and began to think they should have a treaty too. Gov. Joao Maria Ferreira do Amaral, who arrived in 1846, aggressively asserted Portuguese authority over Macau. He closed the Chinese customs house and began developing the land from the city walls to the border gate, plowing up many Chinese graves. He paid compensation but earned the enmity of the Chinese, who ordered their countrymen to close their shops. In 1849 he was assassinated, presumably on orders from Canton, while riding near the border. For many years a large equestrian statue of Gov. Amaral dominated the roundabout leading to the Taipa Island Bridge in front of the Lisboa Hotel. It was taken down in 1992 and shipped to Lisbon to remove the offending figure well before the handover of Macau to China. Nonetheless, the roundabout still bears his name. There also exist a *rua*, an *estrada* and an *istmo* bearing the controversial governor's name. So he is by no means forgotten in Macau even today, or unhonored.

In 1887 Portugal finally got the treaty officially recognizing their presence and permitting them to run their colony without Chinese interference – 330 years after the first Portuguese settlement. Many of the Macanese, even then, believed it was an unnecessary provocation that might come back to haunt the colony. It finally did in 1966-67, when the Chinese Cultural Revolution spilled over into Macau with riots often directed at symbols of Portuguese authority. The following years were trying times. In 1974 Portugal's right-wing Salazar dictatorship was overthrown in the so-called Carnation Revolution. Democracy followed, but not without fears that Portugal – and its overseas territories – might descend into Marxism. Many older families left Macau in those years, emigrating to Hong Kong, Brazil, Portugal or the United States. Lisbon quickly divested itself of its empire and offered to return Macau to China. Beijing said the time was not ripe, and the two sides eventually settled on a formal description of Macau as Chinese territory under Portuguese administration, which in essence is what it always had been.

On December 20, 1999, Portuguese administration ended after 442 years with the raising of China's flag and the establishment of the Macau Special Administrative Region (SAR). The date had no special meaning. Lisbon would have liked to delay the handover until 2007, which would have neatly rounded off 450 years of Portuguese rule. However, Beijing insisted that it had to be accomplished before the end of the century. Macau's return was under virtually the same terms as those that applied to Hong Kong but was accomplished with fewer dramatics. Perhaps the only sore point was Beijing's last-minute decision to station soldiers of the People's Liberation Army in the SAR. No question had arisen over the stationing of PLA troops in neighboring Hong Kong, but Macau had been demilitarized since the last Portuguese troops were withdrawn in 1976. And, unlike Hong Kong, there were no bases or barracks left in the city. The population, however, seemed to welcome the Chinese army with genuine enthusiasm when they entered the enclave. A nasty gang war connected with the casinos had been raging, and the Portuguese administration's competence in maintaining law and order had been called into question. In fact, crime diminished markedly after the handover, even though the PLA's presence has been largely invisible.

Today probably no more than 1,000 Portuguese "metropolitans," that is people from the former colonial power, live in Macau, compared with about 4,000 in the mid-1990s. The Filipino population actually outnumbers the Portuguese by a wide margin. It is often surprising how small this number is, considering the strong Portuguese ambience of the place. Every street, lane and alleyway has a Portuguese name and is marked with the characteristic blue-tile signs. Portuguese-language newspapers are sold on the newsstands. How this tiny community supports two daily vernacular newspapers is a mystery. The Portuguese-language television station is, presumably, heavily subsidized. One of the sights of Macau is simply to see a gentleman from Portugal, perhaps with a dark beard, sitting in the Senate Square, reading *Jornal Tribuna* or sipping coffee and eating egg tarts in the Ou-Mun pastry shop. Portuguese remains after the handover an official language, making Macau the only country in Asia, besides East Timor, that has adopted a Latin tongue as an official language. The governor has departed the gaudy pink palace on the Praia Grande, but the Portuguese Consul-General secured for himself an official residence almost as hallowed in tradition and splendid in style and setting: the former Bela Vista Hotel. The Consulate itself, in the three-story former St. Rafael Hospital, is said to be Lisbon's largest diplomatic outpost. Such a large establishment is necessary, we are told, to deal with the affairs of the 120,000 Portuguese citizens in the territory, a quarter of the population. But, of course, the vast majority of these people are Chinese who have obtained Portuguese passports. On this matter Lisbon was far more generous than were the British in Hong Kong. It is a kind of insurance against the uncertainties of Chinese rule. The "passport holders" will probably never set foot in Portugal.

Somewhat more numerous, but still a distinct minority, are the 7,000-10,000 mixed-blood Macanese. The term refers to the descendants of the soldiers and administrators who came out from Portugal. In the years before the advent of steamships, the colonialists did not bring wives with them and, instead, married local women. Learning to speak Cantonese on the street or in their homes and educated formally in Portuguese, their children became the natural intermediaries, indispensable for the administration of the colony. Over the centuries they developed a distinctive culture that combines elements of virtually all of the peoples living along the South China coast, including Malays, Indians, Vietnamese, and of course, Chinese. The Macanese have their own special cuisine and even a separate dialect, the *patua*, though it is hardly spoken today. Even more than the Portuguese themselves, this community has done the most to give Macau its special ambience. One can see their influence in the numerous Roman Catholic Churches and the number of restaurants boasting of their "Macanese" cuisine which, like the race itself, is a distinctive mingling of Portuguese, Chinese, Indian and other Asian influences.

Up until the late 19th century, Macau was clearly divided into two fairly distinct quarters: the "Chinese city" and the European quarter, usually called the "Christian City". The Chinese city stretched around the Inner Harbour from Barra Point to the Lin Fong Temple near the barrier gate. Its heart was the bazaar, which was mostly destroyed after the turn of the 20th century to make way for the new cross-city thoroughfare, Avenida de Almeida Ribeiro. Today this part of the city still has a definite Chinese atmosphere, with many market stalls and tea houses, especially along Rua Cinco de Outubro. The Christian city, with its Portuguese-style houses, gardens and fruit trees, spread through the city's center and along the Outer Harbour. In times past, this area must have resounded with church bells signaling the Ave Marias at dawn to the Compline at dusk, interspersed with bugle calls from the nearby forts. Of course, the Chinese city has laid aside its geographical limits to share now the whole of the city.

Since the early 1990s the Macau government has been spending millions of *patacas* on preserving and polishing the enclave's Portuguese heritage. You can see the results everywhere in explosions of reds, oranges, yellows and pinks, which are accentuated by being set against the overall gray blandness of Macau's cityscape. Only a few years ago, the Senate Square in the center of old Macau looked decidedly run-down. Not today. It has been lovingly restored. Limestone and basalt were imported from Europe, and some of the finest Portuguese craftsmen brought in to fashion a wavy white-and-black pavement that gives the plaza a distinctly Mediterranean look. The buildings surrounding the square have been refurbished and freshly painted. On July 15, 2005, the World Heritage Committee agreed to inscribe "The Historic Center of Macau" on the World Heritage List, making it the 31st heritage site in China. The historic center encompasses some 30 sites in peninsular Macau from the Casa Garden to Barra Point.

This preservation program represents a fundamental distinction between how Macau and Hong Kong have reacted to the resumption of Chinese sovereignty. Hong Kong worries incessantly about its autonomy from China, which it defines almost totally in political terms, such as the rule of law and democracy. Macau worries about maintaining its own distinctiveness from China, which it defines mainly in cultural or architectural terms. Macau is a small place, and it fears that it could easily be absorbed into Zhuhai – the faceless, characterless Chinese boomtown across the border. The European culture that was brought by Portugal has created a mix that is unique to this area – possibly to the world – and a lot of that mix is expressed in its architecture: buildings that look like Christmas cakes with white frosting trim. In some cases whole neighborhoods, such as along the Rua de Felicidade (the Street of Happiness), have been transformed. What was once a red-light district has been gentrified into a cluster of restaurants, shops, laundries and other small businesses, preserving its Chinese character.

The Macanese style can best be described as European baroque with Asian touches. Some buildings display classical Doric columns while simultaneously sporting the curved roof tiles of the Chinese mode. The brilliantly red-orange Moorish Barracks near the tip of Macau shows considerable influences from the Indian subcontinent, another part of the Macau melting pot. A major departure is the Lisboa Hotel, whose design might better be described as 1950s Las Vegas kitsch. Most restored buildings are not all that old. Generally they date to the early 20th century, or perhaps into the late 19th. Almost nothing remains of the 17th-century city except some temple buildings, such as those at the A-Ma Temple, the stone foundations of the Monte and

Barra Forts and, of course, the
imposing stone façade of St.
Paul's cathedral. Not forgotten
is Macau's Chinese heritage.
Buddhist and Taoist temples are
undergoing extensive renovations
too. These include Macau's oldest
temple, the Templo do Patane,
and the almost completely ruined
Sam Pou Temple on Taipa island.

The government has been
doing a lot more than restoring
old buildings. Even more millions have been poured over the
past decade into major reclamation and infrastructure that has
literally changed the profile of Macau. The old Praia Grande has
been altered beyond recognition by an enormous reclamation
project that has created two artificial lakes enclosed by a sweeping
expressway. The reclaimed land has become a platform for some
of the territory's more bizarre monuments, such as the black,
slab-like gateway to "Harmony" that stands close to the tip of
the Macau peninsula – looking sort of like the black stele from
Stanley Kubrick's film *2001: A Space Odyssey* – and the new Macau
Tower. The 1990s were obviously bountiful years for Portuguese
architects. But interspersed among these monstrosities are some
fine examples of what might be described as "Macanese Modern,"
all erected in the last decade of Portuguese administration. They
include not only such showcase buildings as the new Cultural

Center, but also interesting buildings with more prosaic functions, such as the Firemen's Barracks on Taipa.

After the 1999 handover, Portuguese architects moved out and American casino-resort magnates moved in. In a change probably even more profound than the handover to China itself, Macau invited Las Vegas entertainment moguls to enter the casino sector, the only really important business sector in the enclave, previously the exclusive preserve of Chinese gambling tycoon Stanley Ho. Two new gambling concessions were awarded: one to Steve Wynn of the Mirage chain of luxury resorts of which the flagship is the Bellagio Casino, reputed to be the most expensive hotel ever built; and one to Sheldon Adelson, who replicated his Las Vegas Venetian Hotel on the flat, featureless reclaimed land that is gradually turning Taipa and Coloane into a single island. Stanley Ho, guaranteed the third concession because of his long association with Macau, has not been idle either, building a huge theme park called Fisherman's Wharf near the ferry terminal and several other blockbuster casino-hotels. Everyone agreed that Macau's gambling scene needed a facelift. It had neither the old-world elegance of Monte Carlo nor the exuberance of Las Vegas. Few casinos offered any amusements that could not be found next to the gaming tables or one-armed bandits. No big-name entertainers found their way to Macau. The new establishments have undoubtedly added to Macau's attractiveness as a tourist destination without, it seems, detracting from its cultural heritage or the appeal of the city for those who might want to leave the glitz and glamor to explore the other side of Macau.

The best way to do that, of course, is on foot. Macau is a city made for walking. The town itself is only about seven miles square, and you can easily walk from, say, the Guia Lighthouse overlooking the ferry terminal, to the tip of Macau in one day, taking in dozens of sights. This guidebook is broken into eight separate walking tours to allow you to experience the full flavor of the colonial and the modern city and the adjacent islands of Taipa and Coloane. Public transportation is adequate, but taxi drivers often seem to be deliberately obtuse, unable to understand the simplest instructions in English, even for such famous spots as the Monte Fort or the ruins of St. Paul's. It helps to carry a tourist map and point. Or, get on a bus. Macau is so small that it is difficult to get lost, no matter which one you get on. Next to gambling and heritage walks, eating and drinking is probably the main thing that visitors will remember about Macau. And few would want to leave without taking with them a bottle or two of Portuguese wine, vinho verde, vinho tinto and, of course, port (one bottle per person is allowed into Hong Kong duty free). It is also a café society. Locals, especially the Portuguese, can drink coffee and gossip for hours in open air cafés. This book is not meant to be a comprehensive guide to eating and drinking in Macau. But it will mention some restaurants from time to time either because they are worth noting or because they happen to be a good place to rest your weary feet. The bias is toward Portuguese and Macanese establishments, since they are a part of what makes Macau so unique.

Above all, relax. Most visitors arriving from bustling Hong Kong experience a kind of culture shock. Anyone seeking tranquility and serenity can still find it in Macau, unless the annual Grand Prix auto race is underway or one spends the whole time – as many do – totally immersed in the casinos. It is a city for serious strollers, for drinking coffee and gossiping, for old men playing checkers or "walking" their birds in the parks and gardens. There is a pleasant saying in Macau that goes a long way to explain its relaxed pace of living. *Macau sa assi,* a resident might say with a shrug of the shoulders whenever they come across some annoying or frustrating situation. Translated from the Portuguese it means: "That's Macau."

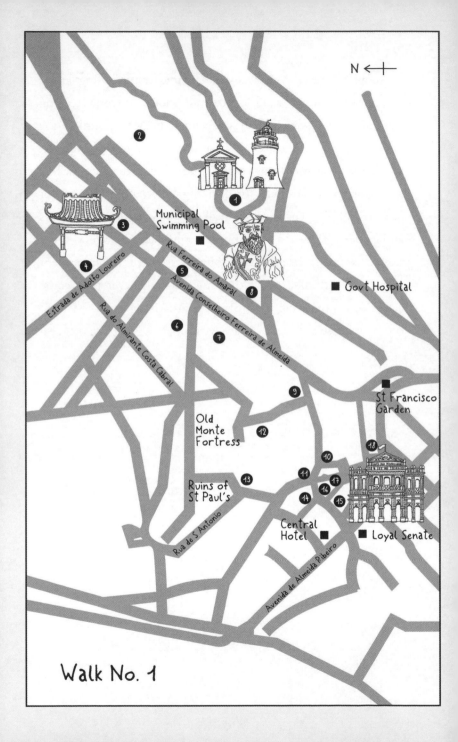

N ←

Municipal
Swimming Pool

Rua Ferreira do Amaral

Estrada de Adolfo Loureiro

Rua do Almirante Costa Cabral

Avenida Conselheiro Ferreira de Almeida

Govt Hospital

St Francisco
Garden

Old
Monte
Fortress

Ruins of
St Paul's

Rua de S Antonio

Central
Hotel

Loyal Senate

Avenida de Almeida Ribeiro

Walk No. 1

From Guia Hill to Senate Square

Route: From Guia Hill through the Floral Garden to the Sun Yat-sen Residence, along Ave. de Conselheiro Ferreira de Almeida to Rua Pedro Nolasco de Silva and on to the Senate Square.

Chief Points of Interest: Guia fortress, chapel and lighthouse, Sun Yat-sen Memorial Hall, Lou Lim Ieoc Garden, Calçada de St. Lazaro, St. Dominic's Church, Lou Kao Mansion and the Holy House of Mercy.

The best place to begin is on **Guia Hill** (1). This is the highest point in the city, and it is a good place to take in its broad sweep before plunging into its details. The easiest way to get there is by taxi. From the taxi line at the ferry terminal you can simply point at the lighthouse, which is clearly visible (but don't be alarmed if the driver takes you almost as far as the Lisboa Hotel before doubling back up towards the hill.) Guia Hill is many things: a lighthouse, a weather station, a restful walking path, but it began as a fortress, and the stone ramparts are still visible. It was built in 1638 in a rough pentagon large enough to contain barracks, water cistern and ammunition stores. It also served as an observation post for approaching unfriendly sails and typhoons. In the 1930s the Portuguese army constructed a series of tunnels under the fort to serve as air raid shelters. They are open to the public and mostly lined with old black-and-white photographs of the army garrison. There were other air raid tunnels dug under Penha Hill but they have been destroyed.

You reach the chapel and lighthouse through a guardhouse, in which are stored the big black metal typhoon symbols – giant triangles, crosses and figure eights that warn of the varying stages of an approaching storm. They still hoist these warning signals on a large flagpole, even if most people nowadays get their information about typhoons from television. But look carefully and you can still see the old symbols next to the number – 1, 3 or 8 – on the screen.

The **Chapel of Our Lady of Guia** was built in 1622. At the entrance on the pavement is a grave with a fine, ironic inscription in Portuguese: *Aquijaza esta porta os christ'por ventura pois nao merece seu corpo tao honrosa sepultura. 1687-1720 anno.* It has been translated several ways, but the gist is this: the poor unknown Christian wretch buried there doesn't deserve such a fine resting place. In those days, returning from a long voyage, a sailor must have looked up at the chapel and said, "Thank God, I'm safe," and then perhaps climbed the hill to offer thanks and prayers in the sanctuary. The chapel has a simple but elegant

façade. Two Doric columns supporting an entablature frame the portico. These elements are repeated around the main entrance. The chapel has been restored in gleaming white and yellow trim, and inside, layers of whitewash and grime have been removed to reveal some rather primitive frescos of cloud scenes, lions and two angels dressed in Asian clothes blowing trumpets. A simple but elegant statue of the Virgin Mary occupies the altar. There are no benches or pews. On the right side of the chapel is the **Guia Lighthouse**, built in 1865, the first on the South China coast. It is 16 meters tall, and its beam can be seen for about 20 miles. The ensemble of the chapel and the lighthouse possesses a great charm. The curved cylinder contrasts, yet complements, the sturdy outline of the chapel. A small restaurant for refreshments is open from 9 a.m. to 5:30 p.m.

From the lighthouse and chapel walk back down the hill and turn right on Estrada do Engenheiro Trigo, a pathway which circles Guia Hill and which is popular with walkers and joggers.

Guia Hill is the largest patch of wooded space in metropolitan Macau. Go as far as the **Floral Garden** (2). Footpaths wind down through the garden, which was built on the site of an old fireworks factory. Nothing particularly distinguishes this small botanical garden. It has a small zoo with a few cages for birds and a Tibetan bear and what must be the world's shortest cable car ride. It starts on Guia Hill and ends near Avenida de Sidonia Pais. The journey takes about two minutes.

Turn left on this street to come to the **Memorial Home of Dr. Sun Yat-sen** (3), the founder of the Chinese Republic. Dr. Sun never lived in this particular house. It was built in 1930, five years after his death. An explosion among nearby dynamite stores destroyed the original house. But it remained in the Sun family and was used as the home of his divorced wife, Lu Mou-ching, until her death in 1958, when it was opened to the public. The gray-brown mansion has, incongruously, many Moorish touches. In the courtyard is a life-sized statue of Dr. Sun, said to be one of only three in China. A smaller bronze bust in the memorial hall is flanked by Nationalist flags that have not been taken down since Macau returned to China. To the left of the foyer is a reading room. Otherwise, the memorial hall is rather bare and scarce on memories, apart from some old photographs and an exhibit of some of his medical instruments – he is said to have been the first Chinese practitioner of Western medicine in Macau. The second floor has Madame Lu's bedroom and a hall for exhibits of calligraphy, paintings and photographs.

Turn right on Estrada Adolfo Loureiro and you come to an exquisite walled garden. **The Lou Lim Ieoc Garden** (4) was built by a wealthy Chinese businessman named Lou Kau. He was born in Sunwei in Guangdong province in 1837 and arrived in Macau in the 1860s, already a scholar and mandarin. He brought with him many of the cultural refinements of his class, including a penchant for private gardens. It was turned into a school and in 1974 sold to the city and opened to the public. The garden is in the classical Suzhou style. You enter through a lovely oval "moon" gate after paying a small entrance fee. I've never been in this park without hearing the haunting strains of the Chinese *erhu* (violin), usually being played in one of the gazebos or on the veranda of the merchant's home overlooking the lotus pond. The estate home, now used as a gallery, is a blend of East and West. Note the classical Corinthian columns along with the Chinese dragon arches at the roof ends. A concrete, winding bridge snakes across the pond, which teems with lotus plants, carp and turtles. The garden is dotted with curious concrete sculptures that look vaguely like lions' or dragons' heads. Enter the park and you feel that you have entered another world detached from the bustle of modern life. Just outside the garden, in a typical Macanese building, is the **Macau Tea Culture House**. This relatively new attraction will stage a variety of exhibitions to promote the study of tea culture.

Leaving the garden, walk down Avenida do Conselheiro Ferreira de Almeida past **Restoration Row** (5), a line of early 20th-century buildings restored in yellow and brown trim. What used to be a soccer field across the street has been turned into a public square. The buildings are also easily visible from Guia Hill, standing out against the dull gray of the rest of the city. These handsome buildings were one of Macau's earliest attempts at preserving some of its older buildings. The work began in the 1970s and set the pattern for future restoration efforts. The outside of the building is repainted and otherwise restored. The insides are gutted and filled with modern appliances, air conditioning, Internet connections, and so on. The buildings are then turned over to the government or non-profit organizations for use, in this case, as archives and headquarters for the health services.

Turn onto Estrada de Cemiterio and walk up to **St. Michael's Cemetery** (6). It has a small but attractive chapel in the center with an ivory crucifix. The gravestones denote the final resting place for many Macanese families. From there descend down a staircase and tree-lined path to Calçada de São Lazaro. This neighborhood near the **Church of St. Lazaro** (7) was developed around the turn of the century as part of a government project to extend the urban area beyond the old city walls to accommodate an expanding population. The streets were laid out in a rectangular grid pattern, giving the district a different feel from the winding, narrow streets of older Macau (the streets, laid out before automobiles became ubiquitous, are still narrow). The whole neighborhood has been fully restored, with buildings in hues of yellow and orange, cobblestone streets and iron gas lights. The church itself, rebuilt in 1967, is not particularly interesting. Climb up the stone stairways and turn to the right for another fine example of recent restoration. The Institute of Social Action is housed in an old Macanese mansion in brilliant blue with white trim known as the **Little Blue House**. Its lack of heritage status prompted the government to propose that it be torn down and replaced with a 14-story office tower. A public outcry forced the government to shelve the plan.

The public park honoring Portugal's greatest explorer, the **Vasco da Gama Garden** (8), can be reached from the Calçada do Igrega de São Lazaro by crossing over to Rua de Joao de Almeida and following this short street to the end. This rather spacious park opened in 1911, and is dominated by a bronze bust to the explorer mounted on a concrete obelisk. More interesting is the bright red with white trim two-story building that stands on the corner of the Rua Nova a Guia across from the park. It houses the Institute of European States and is one of two prominent buildings in the Moorish style in Macau. The other is the more famous Moorish Barracks near Barra Point.

Returning to Avenida do Conselheiro Ferreira de Almeida, turn right and walk to the intersection of Rua Pedro Nolasco da Silva. On the right is the new **Consulate General of Portugal** (9), in a 1930s building that was once St. Raphael's Hospital and later the headquarters for the Macau Monetary Authority. Continuing along this street leads directly to the Largo do Senado (Senate Square). But before you arrive take time to lift your eyes from street level to take in the colorful balconies and windows that decorate the second and third stories of buildings along the way. It is always a good rule when exploring Macau to look up, since much of the interest is in the details of the windows and balconies and the fine iron grilling that guards them. At one corner of Rua do São Domingo is the **Portuguese Bookstore** (10). Most of the books, of course, are in Portuguese, but it does sell some English language books and souvenirs and contains a small downstairs art gallery. Across the way is what used to be a charming little **Chinese cake shop** (11) now selling cosmetics. It is an example of how restoration of some of Macau's buildings has not been left just to showcase government buildings or monuments but also to modest business establishments. From here it is just a few meters to the Square itself.

DETOUR: Turn right on Calçada dos Verdades and follow this narrow lane to the **Na Cha Temple** (12), a small, gaudily-painted bright-red Taoist sanctuary honoring the patron of children. It is located at the meeting of two lanes named after figures from the Spanish epic: Travessa de Sancho Pancha and Dom Quixote. This small temple is the location of a popular ceremony – the stamping of the belly button. In the spring (technically the 18th day of the 5th moon on the Chinese lunar calendar) children are brought to the temple by their parents to get stamped with a big wooden stamp. It leaves a large, rectangular red image on the stomach. This is supposed to ward off demons that might enter the body through this orifice. Leave the temple and walk down Travessa do Penada – through winding back streets with colorful names such as Shrimp Paste Lane (Travessa do Balachao) and Pig's Lane (Travessa do Porco) – to Rua da Palha, which quickly leads to the Square. But before heading to the Square turn to the right. On a side street on the route to the façade of St Paul's is the **Restaurante Yes Brazil** (13), Macau's only Brazilian restaurant. This tiny establishment has only three tables on the ground floor (five more upstairs, but the downstairs has more atmosphere). It is run by Maria Jesus, a native of Goias. The specialty is *feijoada Brasil*, black beans with scraps of beef, pork and chicken mixed in and rice on the side. Also popular are various fish stews and *caipirinha*, a Brazilian drink made of sugar cane rum and lime juice.

THE SQUARE

This is really more like a triangle, with Avenida Almeida Ribeiro and the Senate itself as the base and St. Dominic's Church at the apex. The **Largo do Senado** (Senate Square) is the heart of old

Macau and has received a considerable amount of attention from restorers. It is surrounded by renovated neo-classical buildings and shopfronts painted in rich yellows and bright pinks. Adding to the Mediterranean ambience is the wavy black-and-white pavement. Portuguese artisans were brought in to lay the limestone and basalt cobblestones. Since 1992 automobiles have been banned from the square and side streets, giving it over to pedestrians and street festivals. This is one area of the city where developers have been held at bay, and the original feeling of old Macau is preserved. Near the fountain with its iron globe is a kiosk where one can buy an espresso and while away a pleasant hour or so. Painted green with an elaborate metal awning, the kiosk and others like it in Macau are in the Art Nouveau style of the late 19th century and are similar to those found in Paris.

The jewel of the square is the newly restored **St. Dominic's Church** (14) – the Church of Our Lady of the Most Holy Rosary of the Old Convent of Saint Dominic. It is also known as the "Rose Temple" to the Chinese because the Virgin at the altar is holding a rosary in her hands. The present church traces its origins to the late 16th century, when a chapel was built of wood and earth. At one time, the Dominican order held extensive property, including a convent, in Macau and on the Chinese island opposite the Inner Harbour that the Portuguese called Lappa. Most of the property was sold in the 19th century, and the convent taken over by the government. The exterior is a smaller, simpler version of St Paul's, with eight columns rising through three tiers in creamy yellow with white trim, finely decorated but without the visual narrative of St Paul's. There are three doors made of teak and painted green. At the top is an iron cross. Inside is quite simply stunning. It is bright with creamy yellow colors with white trim. There doesn't seem to be a dark or gloomy corner anywhere. The church is divided into a central nave with two ranks of pews. Balconies run for almost the full length of the church on either side but do not hold spaces for worshipers. At the far end, the altar is decorated with an image of Our Lady of the Rosary holding the child painted in pretty pinks and blues. It is a 17th-century work from Portuguese Goa. On either side are statues of St. Dominic and St. Catherine of Sienna and below the black cross of the Dominican order. On the ceiling is beautiful scroll work depicting the emblem of Our Lady of the Rosary based on the letters A.M. (Ave Maria). The accessories, statues, and fonts are in impeccable condition, as are the two beautifully carved confessionals on either side of the sanctuary. The church is often used as a public gallery for concerts.

Next to it is the **Museum of St Dominic's**, with some 300 works of sacred art. It has three levels with many fine examples of saintly images made by craftsmen from all over the old Portuguese empire. They include clerical vestments, silver rosaries and some paintings, including a fine portrait of St. Augustine, painted in oil on wood in the early 17th century. On the top floor are two bronze bells on wood and iron frames, set in the old belfry windows. They are some of the oldest in the city, cast in Macau in 1807 and 1825. *Open daily, 10 a.m. to 6 p.m. Admission free.*

Directly fronting the Square is the **Santa Casa da Misericordia** (15) or the Holy House of Mercy, and its gleaming white headquarters building next to the General Post Office. The Holy House of Mercy is one of the oldest institutions in Macau, founded in 1568 by Dom Belchior Carneiro, often, though erroneously, described as the city's first bishop (the first two bishops appointed to the post never made it to Macau). This titan was also responsible for founding the Senate and the city's first poor hospital, located roughly where the Portuguese Consulate-General stands today. The charity still runs homes for the aged and the blind and does other good works.

The most interesting feature is the main ceremonial hall on the second floor (the first floor is rented out to a government agency), where the charity board still meets. On the walls are portraits of former Portuguese governors and other notables. The portrait of Martha Merop, a famous 19th-century benefactress, has been restored and it takes pride of place with that of the founder Bishop Belchior. The western wall still contains the curious reliquary that hosts what purports to be the skull of the good bishop (a bronze bust of the bishop is found at the end of the side street, Travessa Misericordia, a charming lane lined with attorneys' offices). There are skeptical historians who dispute the authenticity of this relic, but it has occupied this place of honor, flanked by flags of Portugal and the Holy House, for more than a hundred years. A side room is stocked with glass cabinets full of ceramics, many of them with the Jesuit IHS symbol on them; a few ivory statues of Jesus, such as one finds in other museums of sacred art in Macau; and some Japanese, Chinese and European porcelain. The most interesting exhibit is an old book called the *Commitment of the Holy House of Mercy*, dated 1662. It is said to be the oldest existing document in the House archives. Other than that there isn't much to enlighten the visitor about the history of one of Macau's oldest institutions. *Hours: 10 a.m. to 5:30 p.m., closed Sundays and holidays. Entrance fee 5 patacas.*

The side streets around the Senate Square are worth exploring. Turn off Rua de S. Domingos onto Travessa da Se. Partway up the alley, set among other nondescript buildings, is the **Lou Kau Mansion** (16). Built in 1889, it was the home of a wealthy Chinese merchant named Lou Wa Siu, better known as Lou Kau, and his descendants. Lou was an important member of the Chinese community and a benefactor of Chinese charities in the city. Later, the house was rented out to various tenants. The Macau government relocated the tenants and undertook a major restoration. The mansion is a two-story, block-like building made of cool gray bricks. In its day, officials and other worthy gentlemen entered into a kind of waiting hall called the 'sedan hall' as many of them were carried into the mansion on sedan chairs. This leads to the reception hall where Lou would receive his guests. On either side are separate rooms. On the second floor is the master bedroom and a worship hall. Take time to inspect the detail of the *manzhou* windows made of oyster shells, translucent and pleasing to the eyes, as well as the elaborate moldings above the windows and on the walls. The heavy wooden partition separating the waiting hall from the reception hall can be removed to provide space for small performances such as chamber music concerts.

A parallel alleyway known as Travessa de São Domingos is known for its Portuguese pastry shops, such as **Ou-Mun** (17). It is a good place for a  cappuccino with an apple tart or creamy cake. Close by is **Platao** restaurant, one of the city's better Portuguese restaurants. The proprietor used to be the head chef at Government House, and that's why it boasts a white bust of the last Portuguese governor. Sitting in its outdoor setting, drinking wine and eating African chicken, is a pleasant way to end this walk. This side street leads directly to the Largo da Se, where the **Cathedral** (18) is located. The Cathedral dates back to the early 17th century and used to face south, towards Barra Point. It was extensively rebuilt in 1850 at a time when Macau was at its poorest so it is not as ornate as some of the other churches in the city. It was reoriented 90 degrees to form a square with the Bishop's Residence and another neo-classical building on two sides. The center of the Cathedral front, which has a slightly different shade of gray than the twin towers, is what is left of the 17th-century church.

To the right as one exits the Cathedral is the **Bishop's Residence** and office. The building is honeycombed with archives containing historical papers dating back to the 16th century and vaults filled with priceless gold and silver chalices, miters, incense burners and urns, a virtual treasure trove of sacred art. Alas, the residence is not a museum and is only semi-public. But you can walk into the foyer and look around part of the building. At the front, under a beautiful crystal chandelier, is a broad staircase with a red carpet leading to the second floor. Immediately at the top is a lovely statue of Our Lady of the Immaculate Conception, carved in the 16th century and restored in 1991. Wrapped in a beautiful bright blue robe, she stands on a cloud of cherubs. Off to the left is the original painting of the *Martyrs of Nagasaki*. There are other paintings, including a rather striking portrait of St. Sebastian, an arrow piercing his breast. On another wall is a beautiful *pieta*, once the reverse of a Santa Casa da Misericordia banner.

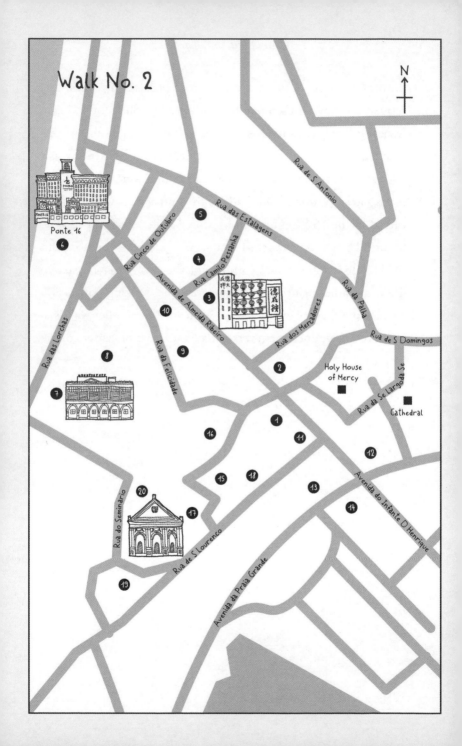

From the Senate to
St. Lawrence's Church

Route: West, then east along Avenida Almeida Ribeiro to the Inner Harbour and down to Rua da Felicidade, then along the Largo de St. Agostinho to Rua Central and St. Lawrence's Church.

Chief Points of Interest: Leal Senado, Tak Seng On Pawnshop Museum, Rua da Felicidade, St. Augustine's Church, Dom Pedro V Theatre, Church of St. Joseph's Seminary and St. Lawrence's Church.

Its building dates only from the late 18th century, but the **Leal Senado** (1) goes back almost to the beginnings of Macau. The local Portuguese community ruled themselves through a local council even before Lisbon began sending out governors. King Joao VI conferred the title "Leal," or Loyal, on the Senate in 1810, honoring its fealty to the Portuguese monarchy during the period in the 17th century when the Spanish and Portuguese crowns were united. Now known officially as the Municipal Council, it still manages the day-to-day housekeeping affairs of metropolitan Macau, picking up the garbage, naming and fixing the streets (the islands of Taipa and Coloane are administered separately). The words "Leal Senado" used to be emblazoned in large letters on the front of the building up until the handover in late 1999. The new Chinese sovereigns would no doubt find it offensive to advertise loyalty to anyone but Beijing.

The foyer is rather shabby, and one quickly passes through it to the small patio garden, which still retains the shape of the patio gardens of old Macau, patterned after those in Portugal and Goa. On either side of the garden are statues of two famous Portuguese writers facing each other. The one on the left is of Portugal's most famous poet, Luis Vaz de Camões and the other of Joao de Deus. On the second floor is a library open to the public in the afternoons. The library is distinguished more by the beautiful ebony bookshelves and a few showpiece books on tables than by its motley collection of mostly Portuguese and English books. Many of them were badly damaged when the Leal Senado was invaded by demonstrators during the spillover of the Cultural Revolution on Dec. 1-3, 1966, known locally from the dates as the "1, 2, 3 Incident." Many books were tossed out onto the square. Until the end of the century, the slope behind the Leal Senado consisted of terraces containing fruit orchards leading up to the church and convent of St. Augustine. The area was dominated by the church's bell tower. Now, of course, the landscape around the Senate is totally blocked by buildings.

AVENIDA ALMEIDA RIBEIRO (SAN MA LO)

The main avenue linking the Inner and the Outer harbours is not ancient. It was constructed only in 1913. Earlier proposals to build an avenue across the city had been hampered by the presence of the large bazaar near the Inner Harbour and by *feng shui* concerns. (It was thought that the road might slice the leg of the dragon that supposedly rests with his head at the Barra point and tail at the border gate.) The street is named after an obscure Minister for Colonies in Lisbon, who gave the project his approval and then was forgotten. Almost everybody in Macau, including local Portuguese, use the Chinese name, *San Ma Lo*, which is more appropriately translated as the "New Street," or "Street of the Horses," presumably because it was straight enough to boast parades by mounted cavalry.

WEST SIDE

Exiting the Leal Senado, turn left and walk along the longest stretch of Avenida Almeida Ribeiro toward the Inner Harbour. Immediately on the right looms the **Central Hotel** (2), its green paint peeling from age. This seedy, decaying old hotel (rooms 150 *patacas* and up) would hardly be worth a glance if it weren't for its interesting history. Opening in 1928, it was Macau's first high-rise building, and more importantly, the first of the casino-hotels which would later reach their full flourish in the Lisboa Hotel and other modern establishments. The *fan-tan* tables are long gone and the Hou Hing Club on the sixth floor, once Macau's largest dance hall, has also disappeared.

Gambling and pawnbrokers go hand-in-hand, providing punters with more cash for the gaming tables after they've gone through the stake they brought with them. After Liberation in 1949 the communists banned both gambling and pawnshops in China as being exploitative. But they continued to flourish in Macau, providing a glimpse of what was once a common element of Chinese culture. A block from the Central Hotel is the **Tak Seng On Pawnshop** (3) at the corner of San Ma Lo and Rua de Camilo Pessanha. The shop opened in 1917 and closed in 1993 and has been turned into a museum. Inside is a tall counter dividing the front from the back area, where the clerks used to work. There is a ticket table for receiving the goods to be pawned. In the back is the storage tower with original safes and wooden cabinets. These multi-story towers, which used to be the tallest structures in Macau, are like fortresses with thick concrete walls and tiny slit windows lined with steel shutters. Lots of people used them for temporary safe storage, and there are plenty of wooden racks to store bedding and expensive clothes.

The rest of the building has been turned into a **Culture Club** in five parts. They include a pastry gallery and arts plaza, selling souvenirs, postcards, clothes and accessories. A third part constitutes the Jin Yong Library dedicated to the famous Chinese writer. The fourth is the Water Teahouse, which provides a comfortable resting spot and a wide array of Chinese teas. The cultural Exhibition Hall features exhibits of Chinese folk arts. Everything is extremely well done, from the exquisite wooden lattice work of the banisters to the red lanterns hanging from the ceilings to the slowly rotating fans; very Chinese retro. The gift shop is probably the most interesting museum shop in Macau. *Hours: 10:30 a.m. to 7 p.m. daily, except for the first Monday of the month. Entrance fee is 5 patacas.*

Tak Seng On is the only preserved pawnshop (not counting the modern ones), but there are others, and it is fun to see if you can spot them. The Tai Sang Tai On Pawnshop at No. 64 Rua Cinco de Outubro is shut down but easily recognized from its characteristic storage tower with the name of the establishment spelled out in big Chinese characters. This street is worth exploring by itself as it has a very Chinese ambience replete with traditional medicine shops, bird's nest shops and so on.

The Cheung Tai Tai On Pawnshop at No. 35 San Ma Lo is easy to overlook. It is a large gray concrete building. Downstairs is now a fish shop. You can still see the storage tower behind the building, which seems to have been turned into apartments. On the large white and black tile sign one can still faintly make out the words "Casa de Penhores (Portuguese for 'pawnshop') Cheung..."; the Chinese characters, going from right to left, mean the same thing.

Turn right on Rua Camilo Pessanha. On the corner is an attractive, three-story Macanese building beautifully restored in green with terraces lined with black iron grilling. This is the headquarters for the **Tung Sin Tong** (4), a charity that is something like the Chinese version of the Holy House of Mercy. It was established in 1892 and once had its headquarters in front of the Senate. The House now operates three clinics, distributes rice, pays for the coffins and funerals of the poor and operates the only free primary-through-secondary school in Macau. Continuing along this street the "look up" rule applies. Masses of pretty iron gratings decorate the second and third floors of these buildings. Turn left on Rua das Estalagens and continue on toward the Inner Harbour. Around the corner, across from a market is the **Kwan Tai Temple**, also known as **Sam Kai Vui Kun Temple** (5), which is formally listed as a World Heritage Site. It is not the most famous Chinese temple in Macau, but it has its attractions. It was originally built in 1759 and is dedicated to Kwan Tai, the God of War and Riches, whose imposing image sits on the altar flanked by images of his son and standard bearer. Two large paper lanterns guard the entrance, and the table for offerings has a beautiful carved front. It was important to the Chinese business community and official edicts from the mainland were once read in front of it.

At the end of San Ma Lo is what used to be the main maritime terminal for the Inner Harbour and, indeed, for all of Macau. **Ponte 16** (6) is where the passenger ferries used to tie up after a leisurely three-to-four-hour voyage from Hong Kong. They eventually were replaced by turbojets, but the last of the class was still plying the waters of the Pearl River Delta in the late 1980s. The old terminal with its clock tower is still there, but the French Sofitel chain appropriated the name Ponte 16 for a mammoth casino hotel adjacent to it, totally obliterating any chance of a view of the waterfront. Across the street is the shell of the former **Grande Hotel.** Built in the 1920s, it was once the height of elegance but is now a derelict. The view from the upper floors offered a nice view of the harbour, which of course would not have been blocked by the new Sofitel hotel. All that is left is the rather graceful, art deco-ish superstructure, which would seem to offer many possibilities for restoration.

Turn left on Rua das Lorchas to the Ponte e Horta Square facing the Inner Harbour. This neighborhood has lost very little of its old raffish character. The 1952 black-and-white movie *Macao*, starring Robert Mitchum and Jane Russell, was partly filmed in this neighborhood. At one corner of the square is a two-story, 19th-century building painted yellow with an arcade running along the first floor and large windows with wooden shutters. This is the old **Opium Factory** (7) where the drug was once stored and processed for local and Chinese consumption. It stood empty for many years and was restored in 2001 under the familiar formula that preserves the architectural externals but turns the interior over to other uses, in this case a medical clinic. (The government presumably does not think opium to be a suitable subject for a museum). Double back up Rua das Lorchas to Rua da Gamboa and one seems to be in another time altogether, a time when this part of Macau was a tangle of narrow, squalid streets lined with opium dens, brothels and gambling halls. The **Patio dos Cules** (8) or Coolies' Patio is a reminder of a time when trafficking in indentured labor was a major activity in

Macau. They were locked up in depots called baracoons awaiting shipment to California to work on the railroads to Peru or to work in the mines.

From here one could continue along Rua das Lorchas until it connects with **Rua do Almirante Sergio**. This busy thoroughfare runs parallel to the Inner Harbour, past numerous "pontes" and ships' chandlers, ending up eventually at Barra Point. Or one could double back by cutting through Travessa Galina (Chicken's Lane) to **Rua da Felicidade** (9), a narrow and otherwise ordinary street flanked by typical Chinese buildings. The name in English – "Street of Happiness" – gives a clue that it was once a red-light district. This street has been thoroughly restored, each of the buildings on either side painted a uniform bright red with gray trim on the second-floor balconies and bright red awnings. In detail these are now mainly ordinary shophouses, small restaurants, laundries and other stores with living quarters above, but the overall effect is very striking. At the far end of the street on the corner of Travessa do Mastro is the original **Fat Siu Lau Restaurant** (10), one of Macau's oldest (founded in 1903). It is famous for a variety of Portuguese and Cantonese dishes, including the ubiquitous African chicken, roast pigeon and *galinha a portuguesa* (chicken in coconut curry sauce.) It now operates two other restaurants in Macau. A few more blocks brings you back to the Senate building.

EAST SIDE

The walk east of the Leal Senado towards the Lisboa Hotel is considerably shorter. Only two blocks separate the Senate from Avenida de Praia Grande. About halfway there, across the street from the Central Post Office (a good place to get some of Macau's attractive postage stamps), is the **Wing Tai Arts Curios Centre** (11), selling paper kites, Shekwan pottery and other crafts. It is easy to miss this store, since it has only a modest storefront. Most of the stock is located on the second and third floors. On the left as you reach the Avenida de Praia Grande is the **Banco Nacional Ultramarino** (12), the national overseas bank of Portugal. It is interesting to note the way the original two-story façade has been preserved and then incorporated into an ultramodern high-rise extension. Keeping the old façade, which dates to the early 20th century, was one of the stipulations made to Portuguese architect Antonio Bruno Soares. The modern extension is set back from the original building, which gives the feeling of a clean-cut separation of the two eras. The colors – lavender for the older part and a vague purple for the glass and aluminum extension – complement each other beautifully and add unity to the building. Around the corner, across from the Statue of Jorge Alvarez, the first Portuguese explorer to reach Asia, is the **Pavilion Supermarket** (13). Its basement stocks a large Portuguese wine cellar with reasonable prices. Across the street is **Restaurante Solmar** (14), one of Macau's oldest Portuguese restaurants.

THE CHRISTIAN CITY

The area immediately behind the Senate Building is the heart of the "Christian City." At least three major churches located close together are a reminder of the importance that the Roman Catholic Church played in the early history of Macau and today. It was here that missionaries stayed, studied and learned languages before setting off for China or Japan. Macau was also a refuge for missionaries and Chinese Christians during periodic pogroms under the Qing dynasty or the Japanese under the Tokugawas. The Jesuits, who came to Macau as early as 1563, founded a college (near the present ruins of St Paul's and Monte Fort, whose guns were manned by priests). It was there that the most famous missionary, Matteo Ricci, studied Chinese before moving to join the Imperial court in Beijing. Many churches were larger establishments than they are today. The St. Augustine Church, for example, was once part of a larger complex that included a monastery and convent. Another large convent once occupied the area that is now the San Francisco public garden but has disappeared.

Begin by climbing Rua Dr. Soares and Calçada do Tronco Velho behind the Senate Building and walking to the **Largo de Santo Augustino** (15). This square is enclosed by the church, the back entrances to St. Joseph's Seminary, the Dom Pedro V Theatre and the **Robert Ho Tung Library** (16). The Augustinians arrived in 1588 in the person of the Spanish Friar Franciso Manrique and a couple of other brothers who founded the city's first monastery on this site. The present church dates to 1814. One of the distinguishing features of this handsome church is the unusual altar figure. It depicts Christ, face contorted in pain, blood already running down his hands, weighed down with the cross set against a kind of diorama of stars in the background. On the first day of Lent, the figure and the cross are removed from their place and taken to the Cathedral for the

night. The next day it is carried through the city, where stations of the Cross are set up in a parade known as the Procession of Our Lord of Passion. Then it is returned to St. Augustine's.

Across the street is the stately **Dom Pedro V Theatre** (17). For many years it was the only theater in the region for a variety of performances and social events. The building, painted green with white trim and classical columns on the front, was built in 1858 and named after the reigning monarch. Old programs and newspaper articles attest to the fact that many celebrated artists performed recitals and concerts of classical music. They included Chinese operas, acrobats and Portuguese music hall performers. During World War II, the building became the home for many refugees from Hong Kong. Nowadays, the new Cultural Centre in the reclaimed NAPE area has supplanted this theater for most performances, but it is still used for smaller amateur dramatics, including some in the local *patua* dialect. The building was thoroughly restored in the late 1980s and reopened in October 1993 with a special revue in *patua* attended by the president of Portugal. The theater is small, or to put it another way, intimate. Only about ten rows of seats face the proscenium and its tiny orchestra pit. The foyer is almost as big as the theater itself. Next door is the Macau Club, where one can see dining the "men in the moustaches" (the Portuguese).

Rua Central is a pale reflection of its previous smartness, when it was Macau's most fashionable avenue. About the only interesting establishment along the way is the **Dom Alfonso III Restaurant** (18), one of the area's better Portuguese restaurants. (It is not named after a Portuguese king; it is the proprietor, Alfonso's, third restaurant). Across the street is a lovely view, looking up toward the Dom Pedro V Theatre, behind a balustrade and banyan tree, which transports the visitor temporarily to a more romantic era.

Follow Rua Central until it becomes Rua de São Lourenço and one can see looming above the street the **Church of St. Lawrence** (19). The first church here was built in 1588. The present one, in a typical classical style framed by twin towers – one with a bell, the other with a clock – dates to the 19th century. The stairwells and tree were featured in many drawings and paintings by the famous London-born artist George Chinnery (1774-1852) who lived for many years not far from St. Lawrence and sketched many scenes. The interior is spacious and richly decorated, with stained glass windows and colonnades with classical cornices. It has a wooden roof ceiling painted in turquoise from which hang elegant chandeliers. On the altar, a forest of silver candle-holders hides the small figure of St. Lawrence. Above him is a crown held up by a cherub.

The **Church of St. Joseph's Seminary** (20) is located behind the Church of St. Lawrence on Rua do Seminario. Approach the church along a sweeping granite staircase that resembles the one facing St. Paul's. The façade, in bright yellow with white trim, is similar to St. Dominic's except it is flanked on either side by towers. On the right (to the left as you face the front) is a bell tower. The bells have been hanging there for two centuries. They were both made in Macau in 1796 by Jose Antonio Pederiva, famous for casting bells and cannons in Macau. But only the two bells of St. Joseph's remain. The church was begun in 1746 and completed in 1758. The dedication stone was discovered during the most recent restoration, completed in late 1999. It attests that "on the 10th of October, 1746, of the nativity year of Jesus Christ the day dedicated to St. Francis of Boija of the Society of Jesus, Bento XIV reigning at Roman See under the protection of the mighty Portuguese King, His Majesty D. Joao V, this foundation stone the first granite stable foundation of the Chapel dedicated to St. Joseph was blessed..." You can see the stone and plaque in a glass case near the altar.

Inside, the chapel is shaped like a Latin cross. It is said to be similar in design to the Bon Gesu Basilica in Rome. The most distinguishing feature is the cupola in the center. The magnificent altar is flanked by four twisted columns in gold gilt and white trim. It is dedicated to St. Joseph, whose statue is in the center.

On the left is St. Inicio de Loyola, the founder of the Society of Jesus and on the right St. Francis Xavier, Apostle of the East. In a glass case, framed in an elaborate silver reliquary just below the statue, is a small bone said to have come from the arm of St. Francis. This holy relic used to be found in the chapel that bears his name on Coloane Island.

There are two side altars. The one on the left, created by one of the great artists of Oporto, is dedicated to the Immaculate Conception and the right one to the Sacred Heart of Jesus. Under the towers are two more altars: one to St. Therese of the infant Jesus and a crucifix on the left. To the right stands Mary Magdalene on a stunning altarpiece. The choir loft has beautiful rows of brown balusters of camphor supported by four twisted columns. Several gravestones are worth looking at. At the center of the main altar is the resting place of Bishop Joaquim de Sousa Saraiva, who arrived in Macau in 1804 to take up his post as Bishop of Beijing. But he was never allowed to enter China and died in Macau in 1818, spending his years teaching at the nearby seminary.

From Lilau Square to Barra Point

Route: Down Rua George Chinnery to Lilau Square, continuing on down Calçada da Barra to the A-Ma Temple, then around Barra Point to Avenida da Praia Grande.

Chief Points of Interest: Lilau Square, Mandarin House, Moorish Barracks, A-Ma Temple, Macau Maritime Museum, Penha Hill, Santa Sancha Palace and the former Bela Vista Hotel.

The name **Rua George Chinnery** (1) just behind St. Lawrence's Church enshrines the memory of the 19th-century British artist who lived near here and whose ink drawings and paintings form the main impressions of Macau as it must have looked more than 100 years ago. The artist actually rented rooms (now gone) on the neighboring Rua Ignacio Baptista, which was close to some of his favorite subjects: St. Lawrence's Church and the Chapel of St. Joseph Seminary. Of course to see Chinnery's most famous scenery one needs to go down to the

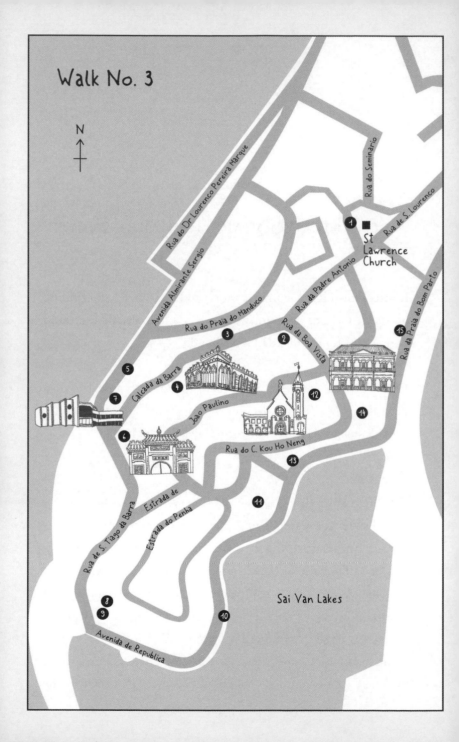

Praia Grande although you will have to use your imagination to screen out the reclamation. To plunge into this neighborhood is a little like stepping back into old Macau, a town of narrow streets, hidden nooks and patios and the sounds of hawkers.

Stroll down this short street to the end and turn left. On one side is the Patio da Ilusao, or Illusion Courtyard, hidden behind a typical Portuguese gateway. Cut through Rua Alleluia to **Lilau Square** (2), the quiet heart of the old Macanese community, built around a fountain. This neighborhood shows the results of considerable attention by the cultural affairs department. The late 19th-century residences on all sides of the small square have been restored in bright pinks, greens and yellows and decorated with black gas lanterns. It is worth pausing for a coffee or cold drink from a kiosk in the square under the shade of a huge banyan tree. The fountain that originally stood in the square was dismantled in the 1940s. The government has reconstructed a replacement water fountain in one end of the square, a large square granite block, which seems incongruously modern in the setting. An old folk poem recalls:

> *Who drinks the waters of Lilau*
> *Will never forget Macau*
> *He either marries here in Macau*
> *Or else returns to Macau*

Just behind the square, down Travessa Antonio Silva, is a building which once represented the height of Chinese residential architecture in Macau. It is based on the design of the home of a senior official of Imperial China, hence the name **Mandarin House** (3). The sprawling complex with nine apartments was built in 1881 by Zheng Guan Ying (1842-1922), a notable official and writer (Sun Yat-sen is said to have admired his critique of bureaucratic decay, *The Jeopardy of Civilization*, written in the Mandarin House). It has been all but abandoned since a fire in 1994, leaving only a few stray cats as permanent residents. Every time I have visited the house in the past, it has been derelict, technically private property, although there was never anybody to stop me from walking in and wandering around. Evidently the details of ownership have been resolved in order to allow the Macau government to take over the property and begin an extensive renovation program aimed at restoring the house to its original condition. This should make it one of the most splendid cultural artifacts in the enclave.

Continue along Calçada da Barra and you will soon come to the **Moorish Barracks** (4), a beautiful public building which, with its Arabian arches, shows the influences of the Indian subcontinent. The 'Moors' were actually Indians from Goa who were brought to Macau to augment the local police and defense forces. It was for these soldiers that the Moorish Barracks were built in 1874. It is now the headquarters for the marine police and is not open to the public; but stroll along the beautiful veranda and imagine what it must have been like to look out over the Inner Harbour before the view was obscured by buildings.

A few more meters' walk brings you to the waterfront. On the left, along Avenida Almirante Sergio, are a row of popular Portuguese restaurants. The first one, **A Lorcha** (5), is one of Macau's better "new wave" Portuguese restaurants with both excellent food and an impressive wine list. A block or so north one finds **O Litoral** and **Porto Interior Restaurants**, both hidden behind fake Macanese façades and both enjoying their own clientele.

MACAU'S LANDFALL

Retrace your steps to the Largo do Pagode da Barra, a pleasant plaza fronted by an attractive green Macanese mansion that used to house the Maritime Museum now located across the street, and the **A-Ma Temple** (6), easily the most famous and picturesque Chinese temple in Macau. The temple was built in 1605, several decades after the Portuguese settled on the peninsula. There must have been some sort of shrine to A-Ma here before then, since it is well established that the temple existed before the Portuguese arrived and that it gave its name to Macau. The name, or a version of it, seems to have been current when the temple was built. It was extensively renovated in 1828, giving it the general appearance that it has today, indeed as it was depicted by all of the famous 19th-century artists of Macau, such as Chinnery and Auguste Bourget. The temple complex consists of four pavilions. The first three are dedicated to Tin Hau, another name for A-Ma, who is the patroness of seafarers and popular with fishermen all along the South China coast. (Approximately 20 other temples to A-Ma exist in Macau, not the least being the imposing statue recently erected on Coloane Island). The fourth and highest pavilion is dedicated to Kun Iam, the goddess of mercy. Numerous smaller side altars are for lesser Buddhist and Taoist deities.

The site is built on the side of a hill, and you ascend by winding paths and steps, relieved at intervals by small temples, shrines and inscriptions and shaded by bamboo groves and banyan trees. Enter by way of a short flight of concrete steps and through a ceremonial gate. In the courtyard is a large rock on which a Chinese junk has been carved in bas-relief. This is meant to represent the ship which, tradition holds, brought the goddess A-Ma to this place. There are various legends. The most common holds that a fleet of junks was dispatched from Fujian province with a young woman on board. A storm arose and sank all of the ships save the one with the maiden. She took the tiller and brought the ship safely to Macau. There she went ashore and disappeared. The other passengers found only a statue of the goddess. On the junk is a flag with four Chinese characters on it; they translate as "crossing the river safely." Progressing up the hill, you pass through an oval "moon gate" painted bright red with nine dragons on the frieze. Behind is an inscription that reads, in Chinese, "the path of enlightenment." Continue upwards past the third and perhaps shabbiest of the three temples to Tin Hau, navigating between large boulders that make the temple grounds look a little like the Camões Grotto, to the fourth and last temple dedicated to Kun Iam, the goddess of mercy. Off to the right is a curious inscription on a boulder in two red Chinese characters said to be a Taoist phrase effective against misfortune.

Across from the A-Ma Temple is the **Macau Maritime Museum** (7) (*open 10 a.m. to 5 p.m. daily except Tuesday, admission 10 patacas*). The museum is attractive and informative, although it depends heavily on ship models and table displays rather than historical or genuine artifacts. Long planned, some of the original exhibits destined for a future museum were destroyed when the U.S. Navy bombed the Portuguese Navy Maritime Aviation Hangar on Taipa in 1945 by mistake. The museum proper comprises three levels. The first depicts, with various models of Chinese fishing junks and examples of fishing techniques, the life and work of fishermen along the South China coast. A model of an oyster field shows growth over five years. Level 2 focuses on the great voyages of discovery by Chinese and Portuguese explorers. A model of a Japanese warrior from Tanegashima, the island off the coast of Kyushu where, in 1543, the Portuguese set up Europe's first trading post in Japan, underscores the importance of the Japanese connection with early Macau. Level 3 explores maritime transportation through various ages: a mock up of a ship's bridge, more models of modern passenger ferries from steamships to the jetfoils, and replicated remains of a Song dynasty Fujian junk. A spacious café with a white tented roof occupies a tiled outdoors area between the museum and the wharf. The museum also operates two junks which make 30-minute tours of the Inner and Outer Harbours (*daily except Tuesday, fare 10 patacas*).

From the Maritime Museum continue walking along Rua de São Tiago da Barra to the tip of Macau's peninsula. There one comes to the **Barra Fort** (8), constructed in 1629 and designed to defend the entrance to the Inner Harbour. It was at one time an elaborate complex supporting a garrison of about 60 soldiers, their stores, cannon and ammunition. In 1740 a chapel was built in the fort dedicated to St. James (S. Tiago). The cannons were sold off to earn money to help care for refugees during World War II. In 1976 the remaining carcass of the old fort was converted into a charming inn, the **Pousada de S. Tiago** (9). Cleverly incorporating the ruins of the fortress, the chapel, the cistern (now an ornamental fountain), and ancient trees are melded into the design. The boutique hotel has only twelve guest rooms, each furnished with antique Portuguese furniture.

Continue along the periphery road, which now becomes Avenida da Republica. This small stretch from the tip of the peninsula to the old Bela Vista Hotel still has something of the feel of the old Praia Grande waterfront as it existed before the enormous reclamation project created the Nam Van Lakes. There are trees, walkways and benches, although the vista across the Sai Van Lake is not very interesting these days. Close to the tip is a **statue of Henri Dunant** (10), the Swiss founder of the Red Cross. It was erected in 1997 to honor the 70th anniversary of the founding of the Macau Red Cross, whose headquarters is located in a fine complex across the street. A little further along brings one to a marvelous wedding cake of a building, in bright pink with white trim. This stately residence, the **Santa Sancha Palace**

(11), was built in the mid-19th century as a private residence and served as the home of Portuguese governors from 1937 to the handover of sovereignty in 1999. The first Chinese Chief Executive of the Macau SAR, the scion of a wealthy banking family, chose not to live in it, preferring his own mansion on Penha Hill.

DETOUR: From Lilau Square walk up Rua Lilau, climb a flight of concrete stairs and follow the cobblestone streets to the peak of Penha Hill. This is one of the two main promontories of Macau, the other being Guia Hill. Here the Portuguese erected another small fortress which was once connected by a wall to the Dom Parto fortress on the waterfront near the former Bela Vista Hotel. In 1622 **Our Lady of Penha Chapel** (12) was also built, and throughout most of Macau's history, it also had a small hermitage for monks. There was nothing much else, the peak being isolated and difficult to reach. The fort was demolished in the late 19th century, and in the 1930s the chapel was totally rebuilt in the form it is today and a small bishop's residence was attached to it. Before the 20th century Macau's bishops had resided at St. Paul's or with churches belonging to their orders. In the 1970s a new residence was built next to the Cathedral, so Penha was used as a bishop's residence for only 30-odd years. It is now part of the University of Macau.

Penha Hill provides excellent views looking out over the city and harbor, but it is a kind of dead place, the quiet disturbed only by the arrival of a tour bus chugging up the hill and disgorging a flock of Chinese tourists. In contrast with the city's other showcase churches, all in neo-classical or baroque style, the chapel looks faintly Gothic. It is stone gray in color, with a tall steeple on one side and an iron compass on the top. The inside is unremarkable save for the lovely oval stained-glass window over the altar depicting the Madonna and Child. From Penha walk back down Estrada de D. Joao Paulino to the pink and white gates of the Santa Sancha Palace.

The palace commands a prominent position in Macau's best residential area. The contour of the land has been unchanged since it was built, so that the building is easily visible from various parts of the city. The two-story building is very pleasing to the eye, having a perfectly symmetrical façade crowned by a curved pediment which used to boast the Portuguese coat of arms, and now the seal of the People's Republic of China. The building is made out of plastered brick in the Pombaline style similar to the Government Palace further down the Praia (which once belonged to the same owner.) Surrounding the whole is a granite wall with Western-style parapets decorated with Chinese ceramics. At the end of the grounds is a circular belvedere with a large shade tree, which must have been a wonderful place to sit on a cool summer's night looking out at the Pearl River and Taipa Island. It was built in typical Mediterranean style with large flowerpots standing on the balustrades. The interior is furnished with Chinese and Portuguese furniture. Down on the Praia is an excellent restaurant, **Henri's Galley** (13). This unpretentious establishment has a nautical flavor – the walls are adorned with a ship's wheel and prints of old sailing ships, oars and signaling flags, and it has a few outdoor tables. The house specialties, African chicken and spicy prawns, are excellent.

The top Portuguese in Macau moved out of Santa Sancha and into the legendary **Bela Vista Hotel** (14), disappointing hundreds of aficionados of what may have been Macau's most beloved hotel. It was built in the 1870s on the ruins of the Dom Parto Fort, the oldest in Macau, whose foundations are still visible from the road. It began life as the Boa Vista Hotel in 1899, aptly named for its incomparable view over the Praia Grande Bay and Pearl River but in the succeeding 100 years underwent several permutations, becoming a secondary school (renowned Portuguese poet Camilo Pessanha once taught there) and a billet for Hong Kong civil service cadets. It reverted to being a hotel in 1967; not the best of times, considering the dearth of visitors because of the violence in the aftermath of the Cultural Revolution. Newly known as the Bela Vista, it began rebuilding its reputation for gracious, colonial-style hospitality, each of the 23 rooms boasting high ceilings, huge bathtubs and a veranda, although the occasional peeling paint gave it a slightly seedy look. In 1990 the Mandarin Oriental hotel group undertook an expensive restoration, reducing the two dozen rooms to only eight luxury suites, earning the hotel rave reviews as one of the world's leading boutique hotels. The last guest moved out on March 28, 1999, after the building was sold to the Portuguese government as the official residence of the consul general.

The rest of the walk provides little impression of the grandeur of the old Praia Grande. Most of this area has undergone massive reclamation in recent years. At one time a row of elegant government buildings and merchants' mansions fronted the waterfront, but the only reminder of its glory days is the red-and-white **Government Palace** (15), which has served as the governor's office since 1884. It was originally a private mansion, designed by the same architect who built the Santa Sancha. The Legislative Assembly moved to new quarters on the reclaimed island on the Nam Van Lake, and the building is now used mainly to welcome dignitaries when they arrive in Macau.

Walk No. 4

From Monte Fort to the Camões Garden

Route: From the lower steps of the Ruins of St. Paul's along Rua de St. Antonio to the Church of St. Anthony and the Camões Garden.

Points of Interest: Monte Fort, Museum of Macau, Ruins of St. Paul's Church, Church of St. Anthony, Camões Garden and Old Protestant Cemetery.

MACAU'S ACROPOLIS

The Monte Fort and the Ruins of St. Paul's Church, the two most emblematic relics of old Macau, are both products of the organizational abilities and missionary zeal of the Society of Jesus. The first Jesuits began arriving in Macau in 1561-63, and they settled around Monte Hill in the middle of the peninsula. They flourished in the new trading town, and by the beginning of the 17th century they had secured a steady income in the form

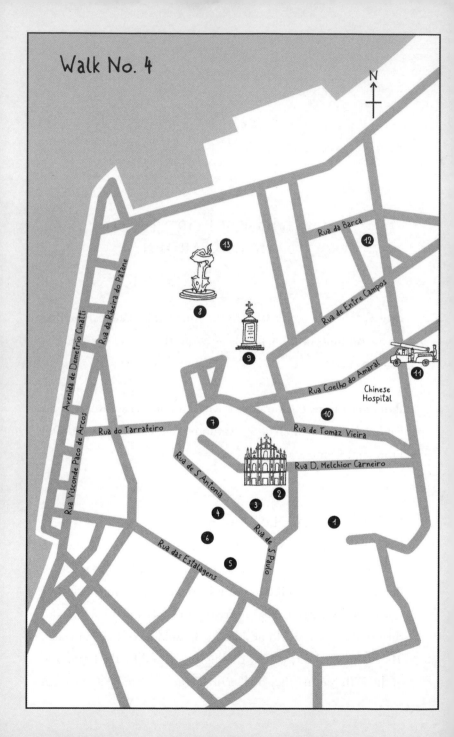

of a tax on the trade with Japan (which, of course, was partly opened due to their missionary activities). In 1594 the Jesuits founded a seminary on one slope of the hill between what is now the façade of the church and the fort. It grew into one of the most important educational institutions in Asia, training numerous missionaries for work in China and Japan. They began building the Monte Fort in 1617, just in time to help repulse the Dutch invasion (the cannons were manned by priests). It was completed in 1626 as noted on an inscription on a stone tablet on the wall of the inner gate. The cornerstone for St. Paul's Church was laid in 1602, but the famous stone façade was not erected until the 1630s. Much of the work was done by Japanese Christian artisans. The fort remained the headquarters of the Jesuits until the arrival of Francisco de Mascarenhas, Macau's first governor, who pushed them out and turned the fort into Government House. It remained the center of government until the late 18th century when the governors moved into new headquarters on the Praia Grande. The Jesuits were expelled from Macau in 1762 and the college was converted into an army barracks. On the night of January 29, 1835, a fire that started in the kitchen of the barracks soon destroyed the fortress buildings, the college and all of the church except for one stone wall. The church was never rebuilt. Only the stone façade remains.

A pretty legend says that much of the vast wealth the Jesuits accumulated is hidden in a secret, undiscovered vault under the broad steps of St Paul's. As mentioned, the Society levied a 1% duty on the value of the cargo carried by all ships sailing into the harbor, which certainly would have been enough to buy a lot of gold and silver. When the Jesuits were expelled from Portuguese territory, soldiers sent to confiscate the valuables found the corridors of the seminary deserted, the famous library empty. Where were the magnificent silver and gold chalices that the priests had used in their services or carried on festival days? And where were the books from their famous library? That gave rise to the legend that the Jesuits had stored their wealth in a secret treasure trove under the very steps that led to the church. Recent excavations have turned up some previously unknown rooms under the ruins but no corridor was found linking them with a secret room beneath the steps. In the 1960s some of the library's books were found stored in the National Archives in Madrid. They had been sent to Manila after the expulsion of the Jesuits, and from Manila they were sent to the Spanish capital.

The **Monte Fort** (1) is made of a gray material called *chunambo*, which is a mixture of earth, straw, and lime from oyster shells that is strong and more resilient than stone or brick. Instead of cracking, it absorbs cannonballs like a sponge. The fort is laid out in the classical style and contains the usual barracks, water cistern, store rooms and cannons (none of those on display are original). Note that there are no cannon ports on the northern side of the fort, facing China. In recent years the top part of the fort was turned into a public park. The only building was a small office that housed the Meteorological Department. Then in 1994 an inspired decision was made to build in its place the **Museum of Macau**. The museum comprises three levels, only

The façade of St Paul's Church is the most important cultural relic of old Macau. A 19th-century fire destroyed the church, leaving only the stone face. It was never rebuilt.

The Church of St. Joseph's Seminary can be recognized by the distinctive bell tower on the right. The bell has been hanging in the church for more than two centuries.

The A-Ma Temple near the tip of peninsular Macau is probably Macau's most ornate and important Chinese temple. It gave Macau its name, from A-Ma Gao: the bay of A-Ma.

Pass through this entrance to the A-Ma Temple and climb the hill behind it. There are four distinct stages dedicated to the patron of seafarers.

The charming St. Dominic's Church is located just off the Senate Square in the heart of old Macau. The Chinese call it the "Rose" Temple because the Virgin Mary at the altar is holding a rosary.

This row of early 20th-century houses on Taipa were occupied by the island's chief administrator and his deputies. They have been turned into museums.

This side street called Travessa da Paixao, near the façade of St. Paul's Church, perfectly frames the old church front with authentic Macanese buildings, flower pots and cobblestones.

The little Portuguese egg tarts known here as *nata* are found all over Macau, but probably the best place to sample them is at Lord Stow's Bakery in Coloane Village.

one of which juts above the park level, giving it a pleasing low-lying appearance. You enter by way of an elevator from the Ruins of the Church of St. Paul and are greeted with a vista of a typical Macanese house, yellow with white balustrades. The first level describes the early settlement and history of Macau, aspects of its fortifications and its key position in the great trading routes of the 17th century. Level 2 describes daily life over the centuries, traditional occupations, festivals, and rites of the Macanese and Chinese communities. Level 3 is devoted to life in contemporary Macau: gambling, culture, and literature. Like the Maritime Museum, it is mainly an educational museum; there are not many authentic relics. But it is very tastefully done, especially the wonderful bank of residential building styles, Chinese on the left, Macanese on the right at Level 2. Outside in the fortress garden – in what must have been a storage bunker, maybe for ammunition – is a smaller museum annex with more information about the fortress itself. *(Open 10 a.m. to 6 p.m. daily except Monday, admission 15 patacas).*

The **façade of St. Paul's Church** (2) rises in four horizontal tiers supported by ten classical columns, five on either side of the center and three main entrances. Above the main entrance is the legend "Mater Dei" (Mother of God), a reminder that another name for the church and the school that used to stand next to it was The Church of the Mother of God. The Chinese name for it is *Dai Sam Ba*, which means the big San Pa(olo), as opposed to San Pa(olo) *chai,* or little St. Paulo, which is used for St. Joseph's Church and Seminary. On either side of the main door is the legend IHS, meaning The Name of God, which is the symbol of the Jesuits. The second tier has three openings and four statues, all patron saints of the Jesuits. They are (left-to-right) Francisco de Borja, St. Ignatius Loyola, St. Francis Xavier and Luis Gonzaga. In the central niche of the third tier is a bronze statue of the Virgin Mary surrounded by angels. To the left is a carving of a Portuguese ship in full sail, watched over by another image of Mary, and to the right a seven-headed water dragon whose head is being crushed by the Virgin. Further to the sides are reclining figures pierced with arrows with Chinese inscriptions on the side. They read: "He who remembers death shall be without sin." And beside a devil shot with arrows: "It is the Devil who entices man to evil." At the center of the fourth tier is a statue of Jesus surrounded by symbols of the crucifixion. On either side are angels, one holding a cross, the other a scourging pillar. Surmounting the last tier is the pediment with a bronze dove of peace with outstretched wings, surrounded by stars, sun and moon.

St. Paul's has been "restored" to the extent that the area behind the stone front has been smoothed over, a crypt for the Christians martyred in 16th-century pogroms and a small museum added near the place where the altar once stood. Nobody, of course, would think of trying to rebuild the church itself, even if full plans existed, since the singularity of the standing stone wall is its chief fascination. The floor of the chapel nave has been paved over to make walking easier. At the far end, where the chancel could be found in years past, is a modern crypt containing the bones of the Japanese and Vietnamese Christians brought back to Macau from their countries. The bones are visible in the stacks of glass tiers. Their names are listed on a metal plaque. A pile of large stones on which the chapel was built is also displayed along with the remnants of a grave for Father Alexandre Valignano, the founder of the college. Next to the crypt is a small Sacred Art Museum, containing a collection of paintings, statues and other regalia of the Macau Diocese. Among the most notable is an ornate silver canopy and a large statue of St. Augustine, a magnificent Indo-Portuguese wood carving from the 17th century that once was in the Augustine convent behind the Senate. The walls display six large paintings, of which the most interesting is that of St. Michael Archangel painted on wood by a 17th-century Japanese Christian. It originally hung in the transept of the church and is the only painting to survive the fire. The painting of the *Martyrs of Nagasaki* is a copy of the original, painted in 1640, that can be seen in the Bishop's Residence in the Largo da Se. Among those who were killed in the persecution was Carlos Spinola, the architect of St. Paul's.

Just behind the ruins of St. Paul's is a small Chinese temple dedicated to **Na Cha** and the only surviving segment of the walls that used to protect Macau. The temple is very small, only about five meters deep. Both are listed as World Heritage Sites, although it is hard to understand why. Built in 1889, it is hardly ancient, but the temple's location beside St. Paul's supposedly underscores Macau's multicultural heritage and tolerance. The wall, made of the same material as the Monte fort, is unremarkable to look at, but it is at least a surviving segment of Macau history.

From St. Paul's walk down a little side street called **Travessa da Paixao** (3) toward Rua de Santo Antonio. This narrow street, with typical Macanese homes on the left, perfectly frames the façade of St. Paul's at an angle. It is a popular place for artists and a good place to take one last look at St. Paul's, and take a photograph, before continuing the walk down Rua de S. Antonio. This cobbled street, and along Rua St. Paul below the steps, is Macau's version of Hong Kong's Hollywood Road. Its entire length is lined by antique, furniture and curio shops. The furniture shops in this area are so numerous, it is at first hard to tell them apart. A little browsing reveals subtle differences and specialities. Some of the owners operate more than one outlet. Among the more interesting stores along the way are **Yu Arts** (4), which has an interesting collection of Chinese furniture. The **Lao Ditan** is a good place to look for Tibetan rugs, and the **Hoi Lung Arts and Trading Company** for classical Chinese ceramics.

DETOUR: Cut down one of the alleys to Rua da Tercena and Rua Nossa Senhora do Amparo for more antiques and other interesting shops in this, one of the oldest commercial districts of the city. Many are outlets for craftsmen making household altars and shrines and other religious artifacts for the many Chinese temples large and small in Macau. Their shop windows display gilded and painted wooden figures, images of deities, incense and incense holders, and paper artifacts to be burned as offerings. A fascinating side street running parallel to Rua da Tercena is **Rua dos Ervanarios** (5). Its name, Herbalists' Street, suggests it was once filled with apothecaries, but now it is mostly a center of crafts, jade shops, makers of Chinese wedding dresses and curios. It is a narrow street, paved with white and black cobblestones in the same manner as the Senate Square. One especially interesting shop selling Mao Zedong memorabilia and other collectables is **Sa Ta Fao** (6) located at the spot where the street rejoins Rua da Tercena.

Rua de Santo Antonio leads, logically enough, to the **Church of St. Anthony** (7). This church stands on the site of a chapel founded in 1558, just one year after the traditional date for the founding of Macau. It is the oldest church in the territory. It stands near what was the northwest gate for the old city walls. The story of the present church is succinctly told in a stone inscription at the lower left base: "Built in 1638; burned in 1809; rebuilt in 1810; burned in 1874; repaired in 1875." A concrete cross in the courtyard bears the date 1636. St. Anthony is a military saint and a "captain" in the Portuguese army. Each year on his feast day (June 13) a ceremony takes place in which the chairman of the Macau Council (Senate) presents him with his "wages" and his image is taken in a procession to inspect what is left of the city's old forts. An interesting figure inside, to the left of the nave, is a Korean. This is St. Andrew Kim, the first Christian missionary to Korea who studied in Macau. A larger bronze statue of him can be found in the Camões Garden nearby.

CASA GARDEN

Across from Largo de St. Antonio one finds the Camões Gardens, headquarters of the Orient Foundation and the Old Protestant Cemetery, which once formed a single unit known as the Casa Garden. These properties, including the garden and rocks, belonged in the late 18th and early 19th centuries to the powerful British East India Company, which also owned or rented prominent premises on the Praia Grande. The **Camões Garden** (8) is probably the city's most famous after the Lou Lim Ieoc already seen. It is however more rustic, a veritable jungle of banyan trees, ferns and large boulders on a small hill. During the day the park is filled with old men lounging on the concrete benches playing checkers, talking with their friends or "walking" their caged birds. Almost from the beginning of the city, this place has been associated with Portugal's greatest poet, Luis Vaz de Camões. In the early 1600s the grotto was already being called by locals the Penedos de Camões, or the Camões Boulders. Whether the poet actually lived and wrote in Macau, as many Macanese believe, can probably never be proven conclusively – the poet died in poverty and even his tomb in Portugal is empty. By tradition, Camões held the position of superintendent of the property of the dead for three years (1563-1566) in Macau. He may have written some of his epic *Os Lusiadas* there too, although there is no specific description of the city in it. But of course, he would have resided there at the very beginning, when Macau was nothing more than a collection of huts on a narrow peninsula of China. None of the famous edifices, forts or churches had yet been built. Since the 19th century a bronze bust of the one-eyed poet has been in a nook of three large rocks, which look vaguely like Stonehenge, along with an inscription from the first canto of his famous poem.

Next to it is the entrance to the **Old Protestant Cemetery** (9) and Morrison Chapel. The cemetery dates from the early 19th century, when Americans and northern Europeans began appearing in Macau in increasing numbers and some of them died there. Where to be buried? Catholic Macau did not want Protestants to rest inside the city walls; the Chinese wanted no foreign bodies profaning their burial grounds in the fields outside of the walls. The issue came to a head with the death in 1821 of the wife of Robert Morrison, the famous missionary, who lived in Macau from 1807 to 1834. The East India Company prevailed on the governor to allow it to buy a plot next to the

Casa Garden, just inside the city walls, for a cemetery. There are about 150 graves, mostly of sailors or family of missionaries. Today the Protestant Cemetery has a strong whiff of chowder about it. Many of the gravestones have good New England names on them – Washington Hickman, Isaac Engle, Hiram Tabbox – as if Melville had written the epitaphs himself.

> *Under this lieth the body*
> *Of Mr. Samuel Proctor of Boston*
> *A young gentleman much esteemed*
> *And regretted by all who knew*
> *Him who departed this life in*
> *Macao, Jan 12, 1792 aged 21 years*

As the date indicates, Proctor was probably buried discreetly in the Chinese area outside the walls and re-interred in the Protestant Cemetery later. The small Morrison Chapel serves a working parish and recently underwent renovation. The stained glass window contains a picture of an open Bible with Chinese characters from John: "In the beginning was the word."

PATANE DETOUR

Walk down the steps behind St. Paul's to Rua Tomas Vieira, and turn onto Rua da Figueira to the **Pau Kung Temple** (10), also known as the Temple of the Reclining Buddha. The temple presents its back to Rua Tomas Vieira, its bright yellow and red exterior to a small wet market. Built some 200 years ago, it is a bustling place, especially around the Lunar New Year when people come to pray to "year gods." The main hall is dedicated to Pau Kung, the Taoist god of justice, originally a Sung Dynasty magistrate famous for probity. To the side is another hall dedicated to Tai Sui, the year god who presides over 60 minor deities, one for each of the sixty years cycle of one's life. People come to this shrine offering paper money, burning candles and incense and praying for a good year. The ceramic statues are of uneven height since they sit on stacks of paper money, the larger stacks seeming to represent the less propitious years, such as the Year of the Pig, and thus needing more divine intercession. Continue along Rua da Figueira and turn right on Rua Coelho do Amaral to the **Fire Department Museum** (11). It is housed in a rather striking, two-story, canary-yellow 1920s building that used to be the headquarters for the fire service. The present fire administration is housed in a new complex immediately behind it. It has a couple of older fire trucks, a collection of helmets and uniforms, fire-fighting implements and photographs of notorious fires. It is a good place to stop if visiting with children. (*Open daily, 10 a.m. to 6 p.m. No charge.*)

Continuing along Rua do Repousa for a couple of blocks brings you to another Chinese temple, the **Lin Kai** (12), facing its own tiny square that is home to a busy flea market on Sundays. Almost every conceivable Buddhist or Taoist god makes his home in one of the several shrines behind the gray brick façade. The main one is Ua Kuong, the dark-faced god who protects against fire. Other halls contain the figures of the 60-year gods and patrons for almost every kind of imaginable distress from marriage, fertility and money troubles to sickness and even dog bites.

Walking down the street, turn left on Rua da Ribeira do Patane. This used to mark the water's edge, although land reclamation has extended the shoreline farther. On the left is a small side street leading to the Largo do Pagode de Patane. Here one finds the **Patane Pagoda** (13), dedicated to the god Tu Di. It looks a little like the A-Ma Temple since it is built against a hillside and the boulders of the Camões Garden. One of the shrines is actually carved into one of the boulders. When it was built in the late 18th century, it would have looked out over the water toward the Ilha Verde (Green Island), now connected to peninsular Macau by reclamation. Now, of course, the view is obscured by buildings on all sides. The side streets leading off from the small temple square, Rua de Pedro and Rua da Palmeiro, give some of the flavor of old Patane, which was once one of the larger villages outside the city walls. The temple fell into disuse and was recently restored by the cultural affairs department. Return to Rua de Ribeira do Patane and catch a bus back to the main part of town.

FROM THE FERRY TERMINAL
TO THE LISBOA HOTEL

Route: From the ferry terminal along Rua Luis Gonzaga Gomes and Rua Pequim to the Lisboa Hotel then along Rua de St. Clara.

Points of Interest: Grand Prix and Wine Museums, Lisboa Hotel, Clube Militar, San Francisco Garden, Statue of Kun Iam, the Macau Cultural Centre and Museum of Science and Technology.

THE LAS VEGAS OF ASIA

The ferryboats sailing into Macau every day deposit thousands of people who ignore the churches, forts and other historical attractions and head straight for the casinos. They leave the casinos only when it is time to catch the boat home or they have run out of money. Gambling has always been popular in Macau, both with the Portuguese as well as the Chinese. From

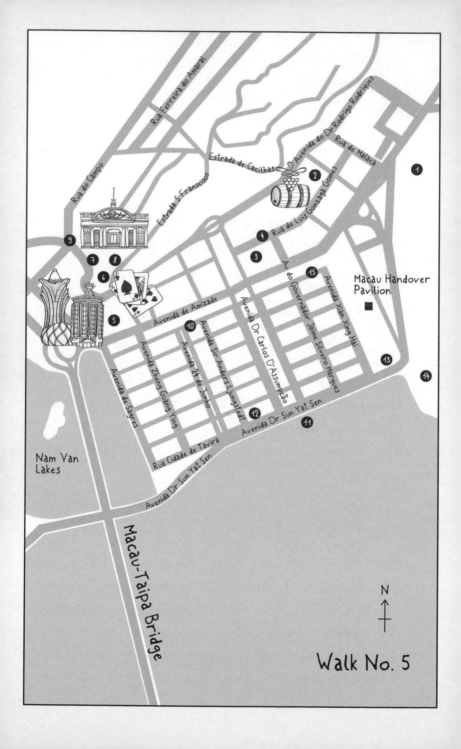

Walk No. 5

the earliest times, Macau had its *fan tan* houses and lotteries. But it did not play such a commanding role in the local economy until the last century. Gambling here got a big boost when Hong Kong banned all forms of public gambling except horse racing, and when gambling was shut down in Guangzhou after the republican revolution of 1911. The first major concessionaire was the Tai Hing Co., which operated out of the Central Hotel, mentioned in an earlier chapter. A seminal day in the modern history of Macau was March 30, 1962, when Stanley Ho went to the Ministry for Overseas Affairs in Lisbon to sign the first concession for his company *Sociedade de Tourismo e Diversoes de Macau* (STDM). It introduced a fleet of fast ferryboats linking Macau to Hong Kong and in the 1970s began building the Lisboa Hotel and Casino. Western games, such as roulette and blackjack, began to complement the traditional Chinese games of chance. The initials STDM were seen everywhere as it became a virtual economic empire. The last monopoly concession was awarded in 1986 and expired on December 31, 2001. The gambling monopoly was broken into three concessions, two of which were awarded to Americans from Las Vegas and one to Ho (who changed the name of his organization to the *Sociedade do Jogos de Macau* (SJM). One thing is certain. Gambling will remain a crucial part of Macau's life and life's blood for many years to come.

Ignoring the new **Fisherman's Wharf** (1), cross Avenida de Amizade and walk down Rua de Malaca. Turn left on Rua de Luis Gonzaga Gomes to come to a building that houses the

Grand Prix Museum (2) and the neighboring **Wine Museum of Macau**. The museum honors the 6.1 km Grand Prix motor race that is held every year in November. (The modern grandstand and control tower are located just across from the ferry terminal building). The Grand Prix Museum has a large collection of Formula 3 racing cars and motorcycles. Perhaps the most interesting, located near the entrance, is the Triumph TR2 in which Eduardo de Carvalho won the first Grand Prix race in 1954. There are also two simulators in which the visitor can get a feel of the race and match wits with other drivers along the circuit.

The Wine Museum next door could be boring for those without a rather deep fascination with Portuguese wine. It is lined with exhibits of every wine-producing area in Portugal with exhausting details of the types of grapes found. There are also some displays of wine-making implements and a collection of vintage wines of which the oldest is an 1815 Madeira. The long wooden tables are a pleasant place to sample wines of considerably more modern vintage. Three wines are included in the entrance fee. More can be tasted for 10 to 30 *patacas* or a little higher for a glass of, say, 1966 Madeira. The museum has an interesting store that stocks many quality Portuguese wines and ports, including some vintages dating back to the 1930s or even 1920s (at prices to match). *Open daily from 10 a.m. to 6 p.m.; a combined ticket can be purchased for 20 patacas.*

Continuing along Rua Luis Gonzaga Gomes, near the cross street of Rua de Nagasaki one comes to a cluster of interesting restaurants. They include the **Porto Exterior** (3), a family-owned restaurant which serves good Portuguese food at reasonable prices and has a good wine list. Across the street is **Patudo** (4), a "snack bar" that is popular with the local Portuguese community.

Cutting through the Jardim do Ho Tim, the street turns into Rua de Pequim (Peking), passing several major hotel-casinos including the Holiday Inn, and leads directly to the mother of all Macau casinos, the **Lisboa Hotel** (5). Apart from the ruins of St. Paul's Church, no structure says "Macau" more than the Lisboa. One can't help but love it, from the sheer kitsch of its design – the neon roof seems poised to blast off into space – to the tawdriness of the interior. Gambling king Stanley Ho built it, so it doubles as a casino. Indeed, gambling is the hotel's reason for being. The rooms are only places where one rests and recovers before heading back to the tables. The hotel has never boasted about its hotel services, which are pretty basic. The Lisboa is a kind of city within a city; its corridors are filled with people 24 hours a day. The hotel has a thousand ways to separate the guest from his money – shops, food stalls, saunas, discos, restaurants, jewelers, antique shops, exotic medicine shops and prostitutes, who congregate around the fruit stall on the second basement floor or patrol the corridors of slot machines. Outside stand numerous pawnshops ready to take the customer's watch or other valuable to go back to the tables. The entrance looks like a large tiger's mouth, ready to gobble up your money.

Stanley Ho began building the Lisboa in the late 1960s on reclaimed land at the bend in the Praia Grande, always a prominent place in the city. The first phase was completed in the autumn of 1970, with 300 rooms. It continued to grow until the last addition was completed in 1993. It now has nearly 1,000 rooms, including 74 suites and 14 restaurants. A considerable amount of Chinese geomancy went into the design of the buildings; noted *feng shui* experts were consulted to ensure that good luck went with the enterprise. The main round building is said to look like a typical Chinese bird cage, designed to hold the gamblers in the casinos until they have left behind all of their money.

If you thought the Lisboa was the height of kitsch, check out its towering neighbor hotel the **Grand Lisboa**, connected to the older establishment by a sky bridge. It is, of course, another element in Stanley Ho's vast gambling empire, and the lobby boasts a bust of the great man underneath a bronze horse's head taken a century ago from the Summer Palace in China. Ho is pleased to tell you that he paid HK$69 million (about US$9 million) for this *objet d'art*, "a world record for a Qing Dynasty bronze." On one side is an encased emerald the size of an egg, and an equally large diamond on the other side. But for sheer crassness it is hard to beat the **Grand Emperor Hotel**, a couple of blocks away. About 70 solid gold bricks have been encased in clear plastic and then buried in the lobby floor so that the guest walks on them on the way to the casino. In all of these new casino-hotels one can easily buy a Rolex from any of a half-dozen watch and jewelry gift shops, but you can't buy a newspaper. The Grand Lisboa does boast in its **Robuchon a Galera** the only Michelin three-starred restaurant in Macau.

From the Lisboa, cross the busy Avenida do Dr. Rodrigo Rodrigues to the San Francisco Fort. The remaining battlements fronting Estrada Sao Francisco form one of the most notorious bends in the Grand Prix race. This spot was once the tip of the wide semicircular bay known to the Portuguese as the Praia Grande, or long beach. Water lapped up along what is now Rua de Santa Clara. For most of Macau's history it was the location of the Franciscan Monastery. The buildings were eventually taken over by the Portuguese army to become the **San Francisco Barracks** (6). The army withdrew from Macau in 1976, and the red-and-white barracks now belong to the security services; the Secretary for Security still makes his headquarters here. In the lobby are display cases of old pictures and prints and other military memorabilia. The inner courtyard contains some old cannons and armored cars. Prominent at the front is the elegant **Clube Militar de Macau** (7) which, as the pedestal proudly proclaims, was founded in 1870. In the late 19th and early 20th centuries it was a social center for colonial society. It went into a long decline, especially after the garrison withdrew. A major restoration effort and member recruitment drive in the mid-1990s has restored the club to its former glory. The restaurant section is open to the public, and naturally enough serves Portuguese food and wine. Try the shredded cod with alumette potatoes mixed with eggs or the seafood stew in white wine. *(Open 12 a.m. to 3 p.m., 7 p.m. to 11 p.m. daily)*.

The San Francisco Garden (8) is the oldest public garden in Macau, first opened in 1864. The original was somewhat larger than the present one. It nonetheless forms a peaceful oasis in the bustling downtown, although sometimes overrun with children from the several schools that are located nearby. The park rises gracefully in wide pathways in several tiers with bright red weathered façades and columns and white balustrades shaded with large trees. At the upper level is a two-story round tower that was originally built as a war memorial and now is the headquarters of the Association for the Handicapped. Engraved on a stone plaque behind a sheltered park bench are some verses from Camões. Walking down Rua de Santa Clara, you will find a small octagonal library called the **Chinese Pavilion** (9). It houses a collection of Chinese publications but is often closed.

NAPESCAPE

The new reclaimed land on the ocean side of Avenida de Amizade, known by its Portuguese acronym as the NAPE (*Novos Aterros do Porto Exterior – New Embankments of the Outer Harbour*), is something entirely different from old Macau. It is a large rectangular pallet of flat land with cube-like offices and apartment buildings with a large green gash of a park running through the middle of it. During the daytime it has a kind of deserted look. But the NAPE has its compensations and attractions which make it worth exploring. Start at Avenida de Amizade next to the towering Landmark shopping complex, and cross the busy avenue by the underpass. On the right, sitting on a marble cube in the aptly named Artists Garden, is a bronze **statue of Jose dos Santos Ferreira** (10). Known by his nickname

"Ade", he wrote poems in Macau's dialect *patua*, full of nostalgia about a dying community. He is a much-loved figure among the Macanese. He sits contemplating life with a small stack of books to one side and his legs crossed, oblivious to the rush of traffic along the busy avenue next to him.

> *The language of the old people of Macau*
> *Will disappear also. What a pity!*
> *One day, in a few years*
> *A child will ask his parents*
> *What is it, after all*
> *The sweet language of Macau?*
>
> — Ade

Continuing along the park one comes to the large **statue of Kun Iam** (11), the Buddhist goddess of mercy and protector of children, who is probably the most popular Buddhist deity. The statue is 20 meters tall and was made of 47 bronze pieces cast in Nanjing, China. It was designed by a Portuguese artist and architect, Cristina Rocha Leiria, which may be why some think it looks vaguely like the Virgin Mary – talk about a fusion of cultures. The goddess gazes out toward Guia Hill and complements another statue of a Buddhist goddess, this one to A-Ma, that was constructed on top of the highest hill on Coloane Island. The Kun Iam statue stands on a bronze lotus pedestal which also serves as a visitor and ecumenical center. It has two levels. The first is a contemplation room. The lower level displays some of the original castings for the statue and has a library and small room for conferences.

From the statue of Kun Iam one can turn to the left and visit a row of bars and restaurants that have sprung up in an area known as **The Docks** (12). Clustered along Avenida Sir Anders Ljungstedt are four cafés or restaurants worth sampling. **Café Marcello** is well-known for drinks and light meals. It also boasts home-made cakes. It is owned by three brothers who were born in Mozambique and brought some African recipes with them. Across the street is an Italian restaurant **Antica Trattoria**, owned by the same people who used to operate the Victoria Italian restaurant near the ferry pier. Next door is **DomGalo**, noted for Portuguese food and with the same owner as the O Galo in Taipa Village. Around the corner on Rua Cidade de Braga is **Carlos** (*Comida a Portuguese*), owned by Carlos Castilho. He serves Macanese food family-style; just ask him what is good.

Or try the Shrimp Diablo with his special sauce. Further south is a cluster of new super Las Vegas-style casino-hotels. They are outside the scope of this guide, but art lovers should check out the lobby of the MGM Grand Hotel, another Stanley Ho establishment, which boasts an original Salvador Dali sculpture, *Dalinian Dancer*. Its Chinese restaurant, The Imperial Garden, is also listed in the Michelin Guide.

Or, one can turn to the right, walking along the waterfront to the striking new **Macau Cultural Centre** (13). It is separated into two parts. On the far end is the performance hall with its distinctive sloping roof which looks sort of like a ski jump. The design was subject to competition and was won by the Portuguese architect Bruno Soares. It has a main concert hall seating 1,220 people and a smaller auditorium for seminars and lectures. In the adjoining building is the **Macau Museum of Art**, which is the city's only public art museum. It has five exhibition galleries, two of them for the permanent collection. Much of the latter was moved from the old Camões Museum after that building was purchased by the Orient Foundation. The "Western" section contains Chinese export trade paintings, sketches by George Chinnery, lithographs by Auguste Borget, paintings by Chinnery's pupil Lam Kua and more modern paintings of Macau by the Russian George Smirnoff. The permanent collection also includes a large selection of Chinese Shekwan ceramics.

Connected to the NAPE by a land bridge is the new **Museum of Science and Technology** (14), designed by famed architect I.M. Pei. Before leaving the NAPE, one more building is worthy of note. It is the **World Trade Center** (15), which stands out from the rest of the crowd of buildings by its variety of different forms in red, black and silver, with the huge letters WTU at the top. Designed by Manuel Vicente, it was voted as the most significant new building in Macau by the Association of Architects.

FROM THE BARRIER GATE
TO THE KUN IAM TEMPLE

Route: Take bus 10a to the Barrier Gate, along Istmo Ferreira do Amaral to the Mong-ha Hill. Turn left along Avenida do Coronel Mesquita to the Kun Iam Temple and on to Avenida Sidonia Pais.

Chief Points of Interest: The Barrier Gate, Red Market, Lin Fung Temple and Lin Zexu Memorial Hall, Mong-ha Fortress and Pousada, and Kun Iam Temple.

For much of its history the northern part of Macau, stretching from the old city walls to the barrier gate, was a no-man's-land except for the village of Wangxia on the slopes of the Mong-ha Hill which was one of the few settled areas on the peninsula when the Portuguese arrived. Its temple, the Kun Iam Temple, is said to date back as far as the Yuan Dynasty (1279 1368), though the present complex was constructed in the 17th century. The

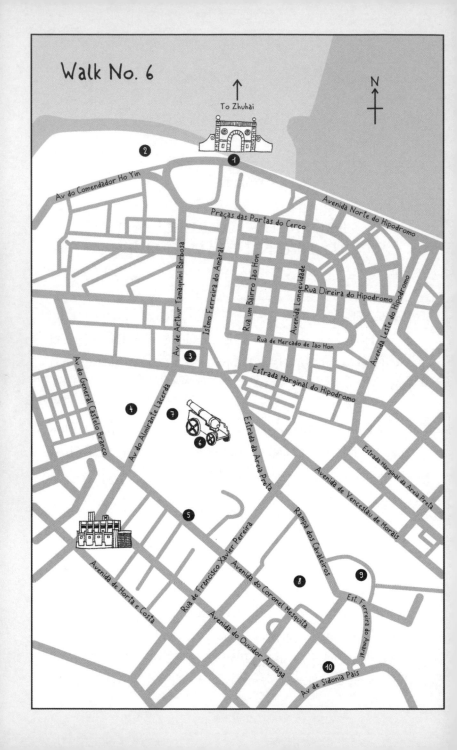

Walk No. 6

To Zhuhai

N

Av do Comendador Ho Yin

Avenida Norte do Hipodromo

Praças das Portas do Cerco

Av de Arthur Tamagnini Barbosa

Istmo Ferreira do Amaral

Rua um Bairro Iao Hon

Avenida Longevidade

Rua Direira do Hipodromo

Avenida Leste do Hipodromo

Rua de Mercado de Iao Hon

Av do General Castelo Branco

Av de Almirante Lacerda

Estrada Marginal do Hipodromo

Estrada da Areia Preta

Estrada Marginal da Areia Preta

Avenida de Venceslau de Morais

Avenida de Horta e Costa

Rua de Francisco Xavier Pereira

Avenida do Coronel Mesquita

Rampa dos Cavaleiros

Avenida do Ouvidor Arriaga

Est. Ferreira do Amaral

Av de Sidonia Pais

configuration of the land then was more like a leaf with a narrow isthmus as a stem. So, it was an obvious place to put a gate, and the Chinese authorities erected one in 1573 designed to keep the Portuguese contained in their enclave at the tip of the peninsula. The Portuguese used the area for picnics, swimming at the beaches and on the Ilha Verde – then detached – and for second homes; the Chinese grew vegetables there and buried their dead. The Portuguese began to assert sovereignty over the area in the mid-19th century when Gov. Ferreira do Amaral built a proper road to the border, cutting through some grave sites. Angry Chinese murdered the governor as he was riding along the road near the border. Today the area is totally urban, more like Kowloon than old Macau. Even the few vegetable gardens have disappeared. Land reclamation has obliterated the old isthmus, presenting a broad land front along the border.

Take bus 10a from the ferry terminal to the **Barrier Gate** (1), known in Portuguese as the *Portas de Cerco*. This is a bustling, chaotic and graceless place. There is nothing like the serenity one sees in old photographs or paintings. Hundreds of automobiles and trucks line up to enter China, while pedestrians stream by the thousands into or out of China past the old gate through the gargantuan customs shed. The Barrier Gate itself looks vaguely like the Arc de Triomphe. The Chinese and Macau SAR flags now fly from the flagpole where once the Portuguese flag proudly demarcated the border. On the lintel are the Portuguese words for "Honor the Fatherland for the Fatherland sees you." This particular structure was erected in the 1870s. The dates of August

22, 1849, on one leg and August 25 on the other refer to the days that Gov. Ferreira do Amaral was assassinated by Chinese patriots near the gate and to a pre-emptive raid across the border by Macanese militia. Army and navy emblems complement the overall military ambience of the structure.

Not far away, to the left of the gate, an extensive slice of reclaimed land has been turned into a public park. **The Sun Yat-sen Memorial Park** (2) opened in 1990 and is a pleasant oasis of peace in a rather chaotic neighborhood, but it offers relatively little of interest to the visitor aside from some views across into China. It does have an aviary made of pyramidal structures, a greenhouse, a small library and a nice little Portuguese restaurant called the **Canal dos Patos** next to a pond with a winding bridge across it made to look like some kind of modern Suzhou garden.

Walk down the bustling Istmo Ferreira do Amaral to the **Lin Fung Temple** (3). It is located at the northern base of the Mong-ha Hill across from an expressway. Note the rather interesting police station on the other side. Dating from 1592, the Lin Fung Temple got its name from the layout of old Macau, which then resembled a lotus leaf. It stands near what used to be the narrow isthmus leading to the border, and its location near the stem made it a convenient way-station and temporary headquarters for visiting Chinese officials. The most important visitors were Commissioner Lin Zexu and the Viceroy of Guangdong and Guangxi provinces, Deng Tuizhen, who arrived on September 3, 1839, on a mission from the Emperor to try to stamp out the opium trade in southern China. He came to the Lin Fung Temple with a complement of troops and was met by a contingent of Portuguese troops. There he conferred with leading Macanese citizens and the Portuguese Governor Silveiro Pinto, seeking Macau's neutrality in the looming hostilities with Britain and sought their cooperation in suppressing the opium trade. By all accounts, the meeting was cordial. Gifts were exchanged, the Monte Fort fired a salute and Lin and his entourage then took a tour of Macau.

The temple has a wide courtyard with a large bronze pagoda in the middle. It has a fine façade of intricate clay bas-relief, depicting historical and mythological figures. The interior is quite large, with half a dozen altars devoted to the Tin Hau and Kun Iam deities and to a couple of lesser ones. Some of the statues are quite elaborate, one with two sets of eyes. The main hall has an interesting square atrium with a raised stone platform and stone railing and a lot of very nice woodwork depicting clouds and dragons. A picture in the nearby **Lin Zcxu Mcmorial Hall** suggests that the famous meeting between Lin and the Macanese took place on this atrium. A concrete statue of the mandarin stands outside the new museum dedicated to his visit. Created by the Lin Fung Temple Charity Association and opened in 1997, the museum is a little amateurish and not very informative for people who do not read Chinese. At the center is a wax tableau meant to depict Lin meeting with the Portuguese officials. There are models of Chinese war junks, an opium warehouse ship and some opium implements. Probably the most interesting artifact is Lin's report to the Emperor of his southern tour. (*Open daily, 9 a.m. to 5 p.m. Entry 10 patacas*).

Walk down Avenida do Almirante Lacerda past the dog racing track to the **Red Market** (4) at the corner of Avenida de Horta e Costa. Macau has half a dozen public wet markets, but the three-story, red-brick market here is probably the most interesting. It was opened in 1936 and is listed officially as an architecturally significant site. It says something about the extent of land reclamation in this part of Macau that it once fronted the water, taking on fresh fish straight from fishermen and vegetables from surrounding farms. In addition to the usual wet market fare of seafood and produce, it has a great Thai food stall and other stalls that sell Indonesian and Malaysian food and ingredients.

Double back on Avenida do Admiralte Lacerda to **Avenida do Coronel Mesquita** (5). The avenue was named after Colonel Nicolau de Mesquita, a Macau-born Portuguese army officer who led a storming party against the Chinese fortress of Passaleao opposite the barrier gate three days after the governor was assassinated. There used to be a statue to Mesquita in the Senate Square, but it was toppled by mobs during the "1, 2, 3 Incident" in December 1966 and never replaced. You can catch a glimpse of the statue if you carefully watch the historical black-and-white film of pre-war Macau at the Museum de Macau. Despite his victory as a young lieutenant, Mesquita was passed over for promotion, presumably because he was of mixed descent. He later went insane and murdered his wife and child before killing himself. Still, he is remembered in Macau with the street name (there is one on Taipa Island too). He rests in St. Michael's Cemetery. His tomb, just to the left of the entrance, bears a bust of the colonel in full uniform with the inscription "Heroic defender of Macau."

Further down the avenue, past the little Kun Iam Temple with a very ornate figure on the altar, is the entrance to Mong-ha Hill. (Mong-ha, which means "dreaming of Amoy" – modern Xiamen – because it was initially populated with people from that city, is also a generic name for all of northern Macau.) Walk up the hill past the modern-looking Institute of Tourism Education, where the Portuguese army had barracks as late as the 1960s. The **Pousada da Mong-ha** (6) is used to visiting professors and other official guests, but it is open to the public and offers a dinner buffet every Friday at reasonable prices. The dining room is paved with red tiles and the walls are lined with typical Portuguese blue and white tiles. The menu rotates over a five-week period. Continuing up the path one comes to the **Fortress of Mong-ha** (7). These guns, unlike at the other Macau forts, were pointed directly at China and not designed to repel European invaders. The Mong-ha was fortified in the 19th century, when Portugal was asserting its sovereignty over the colony and preparing for a Chinese invasion. Completed in 1866, the fort is more like a gun emplacement. It has a more modern look than Macau's other fortresses, being made out of concrete, not *chunambo*. The two 18th-century cannons are too old for the setting and are not original. The Mong-ha has plenty of leafy trails for joggers, with lots of spots to exercise and inspect the plants growing in large greenhouses, and a nice view of the city toward the Barrier Gate and beyond.

Doubling back to Avenida do Coronel Mesquita, one comes to the long green façade of the **Kun Iam Tong Temple** (8). This temple, dedicated to the Buddhist goddess of mercy, is probably the oldest in Macau. It was situated in the village of Wangxia, another name for Mongha, which was the largest settlement on the peninsula when the Portuguese arrived.

In layout it is similar to the Lin Fong Temple. You enter through a large gate into a spacious courtyard planted with banyan trees. Steps lead up to the main hall. Note the exquisite detail of the tile roofs and the porcelain figures on them. In the first hall of the main building are seated three gilded Buddhas. These are the Precious Buddhas of the Realm of the Western Heaven. On either side are passages leading to the next hall that is dedicated to the Buddha of Longevity. On the wall facing the altar is a painted relief depicting dragons coiling through clouds. Passages lead to the third and largest hall, with a profusion of potted lotus plants, and coils of incense burners hanging from the ceiling like beehives. At the center is the goddess of mercy heavily clad in embroidered robes. Behind glass cases are seated Bodhisattvas, the saints of Buddhism. On either side of the main hall are several halls containing spirit tables of deceased parishioners and scrolls honoring Kun Iam in pictures and calligraphy.

Behind the temple is a garden with a small round stone table on which was signed on July 3, 1844, the Treaty of Wangxia, the first treaty between the United States and China. The trade treaty was made by Caleb Cushing from the U.S. and a representative of the Manchu dynasty and the viceroy of Guangdong. It came a couple of years after the end of the first Opium War and the founding of Hong Kong, and the Chinese were keen to use Macau in its traditional role as a meeting place with the outside world. Chinese ink orchids bloom in green-glazed pots, and their scent is overwhelming. Highly fragrant osmanthus also grows there, as do pink, white and red camellias.

Behind the temple is the **Garden of Montanha Russa** (9), next to the New Protestant Cemetery. A spiral trail leads to the top of Russa Hill (russa means "snail") surrounded by a profusion of tropical and European trees.

Continue down Estrada Ferreira do Amaral past the roundabout and one comes to what is generally considered the most authentic Macanese restaurant in the city. **The Riquexo Restaurant** (10) is located in a nondescript shopping center at 69 Avenida Sidonia Pais on top of a Park 'n Shop supermarket. It is a self-service canteen with about a dozen tables and a bar (the Portuguese restaurant and bar next door is not connected). You line up with a tray, cafeteria-style. If you have trouble finding the place, just stand outside on the street at lunchtime and follow the flow of Portuguese-looking patrons. The place is extremely popular with the local Portuguese and Macanese community. It has no need to cater to tourists, is not especially tourist-friendly and is seldom mentioned in Macau promotional materials. It serves basic food like your (Macanese) grandma used to make.

Walk No. 7

TAIPA ISLAND

Route: Take bus 28a from the ferry terminal to Taipa Village, walk along Rua Correia da Silva to the United Chinese Cemetery and take the bus back to Macau.

Chief Points of Interest: Taipa Village, Pak Tai Temple, the Church of Our Lady of Carmel, the Taipa House Museum and Taipa Fort.

The smaller of Macau's two outlying islands, Taipa has much of Macau's modern infrastructure: its airport, university, racetrack and stadium and a growing "new town" in the middle of it. But it also has village streets that are reminiscent of old Macau, a baroque church, another statue to the poet Camões and Chinese temples, no fewer than nine of them. Taipa was originally three small islands that have been stitched together through land reclamation. The two wooded hilltops – Taipa Grande near the airport and Taipa Pequena near the old bridge

– and the Kun Iam rock where the university is located are what used to be the islands.

Taipa entered into the Macanese conscience in the early 18th century when trading ships, denied entry into Guangzhou, anchored in the waters between Taipa and Coloane, now virtually all reclaimed land. It wasn't until the 19th century that the Portuguese began to look at the outlying islands as permanent possessions. Gov. Ferreira do Amaral established a fort on Taipa Pequena in 1847, effectively annexing it. A successor claimed Taipa Grande and soon thereafter Coloane was added. By 1872 a civil administration had been established for the two islands. The treaty with China in 1887 confirmed Portugal as the sovereign of Macau "and its dependencies." The indistinct wording would cause trouble, as Portugal also vaguely claimed three other adjacent islands now in China. As late as World War II, a detachment of Portuguese soldiers occupied the island opposite Macau they called Lappa, but were chased away by Chinese troops after a brief skirmish. The leader, Lt. Alberto Ribeiro da Cunha's name is remembered in the main street of Taipa Village.

The best place to start is Vila de Taipa, the old village. Alight from the bus at the stop opposite the **Tin Hau Temple** (1), another of the many temples to the ubiquitous patron of seafarers. The original temple was built in 1785. It was rebuilt in 1833 with money donated by the families of victims of Chinese pirates. Only one of the three original pavilions remains as a sanctuary. One other was rented to a Chinese restaurant. Across the street in a green-colored old colonial-style mansion is the headquarters of the **Islands Municipal Council** (2), which used to be the town hall of Taipa and Coloane and is now a museum dedicated to the history of Macau's outlying islands.

Entering the old town is like entering a living maze. The streets are narrow, with shops on the ground level, their doors open and the clattering of mahjong players emanating from them. This is a living village. The houses, though in good condition, have not been meticulously restored. The streets do not get much sunlight, but the atmosphere is bright because of the brilliant shades of yellow, green and red on the buildings. Begin at the small square behind the town hall. It is known as Camões Square but it is dominated by the **Pak Tai Temple**. This is dedicated to the Taoist deity, the God of the North. The temple dates to 1844, has been restored twice, most recently in 1994, and has been declared an historical heritage monument. Note the beautifully detailed frieze on the edge of the roof at the entrance. Inside a small skylight dramatically casts a ray of light on the smoke of burning incense spiraling upwards.

Taipa Village is honeycombed with small, intimate restaurants, save for **Pinocchio's**. It serves excellent Portuguese food, but the atmosphere is loud and more Chinese than European. It occupies a large three-story, barn-like building with bare, circular tables. For a more intimate, homey European atmosphere try **Antonio's** located on Rua dos Negociantes. Run by Antonio Neves Coelho, a former cook in the Portuguese army, it offers authentic Portuguese food in a setting large enough for a dozen customers. A large painting on one wall celebrates the beginning of the *fado*.

It rates a star in the Michelin Guide, the only one for a single-owner restaurant in Macau; the other two are part of massive hotel-casino resorts. A few houses down the street is **Taverna**, a nice British-style pub, and around the corner is **A Petisqueira**, another Portuguese restaurant. Along Rua do Cunha, the village's main street, are two other intimate restaurants. At **O Santos**, pennants and pictures of ships on the wall conform to the taste of the proprietor, Santos Manuel Bruno, a former cook in the Portuguese navy, who is usually hovering around ready to help with your choices. Another notable Portuguese-style restaurant is the **O Galo**. Replicas of the ubiquitous Portuguese rooster (*galo*) in all shapes and sizes decorate the walls and shelves.

PRAIA CAUSEWAY

Across from the old village is an entirely different world. The 19th-century church, park and row of Macanese bungalows make this one of the most charming quarters of Macau. From Rua Correia da Silva turn up Calçada do Quartel. The name of the lane, "quarters", is a clue that the Portuguese once had a small military barracks in what is now a police station. Walk up the hill to Largo do Carmo. On the right is the **Church of our Lady of Carmel** (3), built in 1885 and the only Catholic church on Taipa. It is an attractive, two-story structure painted in yellow with white trim with a square bell tower at the top. The interior is bright and comfortable with a well-designed choir stall. To the right of the altar is a statue of Joseph the carpenter. To the left is a statue of the resurrected Jesus, his wounds clearly showing. Facing the church across the square is a beautiful little building with a colonnade of classical columns, once a school, now a public library. Below the church and behind the library is a public park. At the top lookout the government recently erected another statue to Portugal's poet laureate Luis Vaz de Camões.

The esplanade facing the praia used to be a popular beach, and in the 1920s there was located near here a hangar housing seaplanes that used to fly between Macau and Hong Kong. Along with a naval detachment, it was the only Macau aviation unit until the opening of the airport in the 1990s. Construction of the Taipa-Coloane Causeway in 1968 cut off the flow of water, and the beach became a marshland. Behind the esplanade is a row of five green villas known collectively as the **Taipa House Museum** (4). These stately dwellings, all built in 1921, once housed the chairman of the Islands Council and his principal assistants. The chairman lived in the one closest to the church until the late 1990s, after which all five were carefully restored and museumized. The most interesting is the house museum showing how a prosperous Portuguese family lived in the 1920s. Tall, leafy banyan trees line the esplanade, adding to the area's charm and making it a popular and picturesque setting, not only for tourists but also for wedding parties and occasionally as a backdrop for period movies.

The view today across what used to be a wide expanse of water toward Coloane Island would confound any former tenant if he or she should happen to return. The waterfront has shrunk to a small marshy pond. What was once a causeway connecting the two islands has been widened, filled in and turned into a broad, flat pallet of land known as **Cotai** (Coloane-Taipa). Las Vegas and other big hotel interests have built half a dozen massive casino-resorts of which the most massive by far is the **Venetian**, which replicates the one in Las Vegas. Most of these are concentrated for now at the Taipa end of Cotai and, indeed, it is becoming difficult to determine where Taipa leaves off and Cotai begins.

Walk back up to the square and down a tree-shaded lane called Calçada do Canno to Avenida Direita Carlos Eugenio and turn right. You soon come to the **Sam Pou Temple**, striking in its yellow exterior. It was erected in 1843 and lately fell into disrepair. Only recently has it been restored by the Macau Cultural Institute. The goddess Sam Pou is a sister of the ubiquitous Tin Hau and like her is worshiped for her miracles in protecting fishermen and other seafarers. Inside is a beautifully carved reliquary used in festivals. Across the street are the ruins of the **Iec Long Fireworks factory**, a reminder that fireworks manufacture once formed the main industry of Taipa. There are no more "*fabrica de panchoes*" left on Taipa. Continue along the street past the **O-Manel** restaurant to a roundabout. Bearing to the right along the base of Taipa Grande Hill brings you the **United Chinese Cemetery** (5), the largest of Taipa's eight cemeteries (one of the most unusual is reserved for victims of fireworks plant explosions.) Notice the tall concrete statue to the god Tou Tei at the entrance, which at 9 meters used to be the tallest in Macau until the recent building of the A-Ma statue on Coloane and the Kun Iam bronze statue in Macau proper. Exiting the cemetery, take bus 11 back to Macau.

NORTHERN SHORE

It is hard to believe that the former Hyatt Regency Hotel (now the Regent) near the university used to be the height of luxury in Macau. Now the hotel is literally overshadowed by the huge **Altira Hotel** nearby. It has its own restaurants, but one can't help but regret the loss of the old Flamingo. The Taipa Pequena Hill overlooking the bridge has been nicely developed with trail walks and a lookout gazebo that provides a panoramic view across the water. At the base of the hill is a white, high relief concrete **Mural** (6), depicting scenes from Macau life. The structure zigzags its way up the hill in six panels. Portuguese sculptor Dorita Castel Bravo designed it in 1984.

The Pou Tai Un Monastery (7) is easy to spot at the base of the hill with its tall, copper-colored tile roof sticking up among the nearby buildings. This is the largest and possibly the best tended Chinese temple in Macau. It was originally called the Garden of Pou Tai, and was built by the Lo family, one of whom, Lo Pou San, was one of Guangdong's most famous painters. After he died, his son split the property and sold one of the parcels to the Buddhist Master Monk Sik Chi Un, who turned it into a temple. The main pavilion rises three stories high in the middle of the courtyard. A 5.4-meter bronze Buddha sits on an elegant wooden pedestal. An ornate incense burner, looking like a Shang Dynasty bronze wine vessel, is placed in front. On the ground floor is a statue of Kun Iam, represented with 42 arms. The monastery also has a well-regarded vegetarian restaurant that is open to the public.

Continue down Estrada Lou Lim Ieoc, past some rather handsome private mansions with very ornate gates, to a roundabout by a filling station. On the far side is the **Taipa Fort** (8). It was built in 1847 at the request of local people who wanted protection against pirates and because the governor wanted to assert Portuguese sovereignty over Taipa. On top of the fortifications is an attractive, single-story canary-yellow building. It has been variously used as the governor's summer residence, as a police station and now as the headquarters for the Boy Scouts. The exterior looks out over the water towards China with a porch supported by six colonnades and bearing a large Portuguese coat of arms. Adjacent to the fort is an attractive garden, the Jardim do Cais (pier garden – it's next to the old ferry terminal). Walk along Estrada Governador Albano Oliveira past the Jockey Club and the statue of the **Buddha with Four Faces** (9) and follow Avenida de Kwong Tung back to the old Hyatt.

A short walk from the Regent, past the Century Hotel, brings one to **Cheok Ka Village** (10), a tiny hamlet once inhabited by families surnamed Cheok. Today it looks more like a squatters' village, but it does have two small Chinese temples of some interest. One, the Mou Tai Temple, is dedicated to Kuan Tai, once a heroic general in the Han dynasty who, after his death, became a popular deity known as the Sovereign of War. The other is another Tin Hau Temple, dedicated to the familiar protector of seamen. Formerly the two Tin Hau temples on Taipa were located at the northern and southern ends of the watercourse separating Taipa Pequena from Taipa Grande and giving fishermen double protection as they sailed out to sea. Now land reclamation has filled those waters and the northern Tin Hau Temple is almost totally lost among all the high-rises. There is also a small temple dedicated to Kun Iam near the university. Before leaving Taipa, it is worth walking to the Sun Yat-sen Roundabout. On the right is the **Taipa Firemen's Barracks**, a nice example of modern Macanese architecture.

Coloane Island

Route: Take a bus to Coloane Village, walk along Rua dos Navegantes to the old ferry terminal, then along Avenida Cinco de Outubro to the Tam Kung Temple and along Rua do Estaleiro back to the village square.

Chief Points of Interest: Coloane Village, Lord Stow's Bakery, Chapel of St. Francis Xavier, Tam Kung Temple, Seac Pai Van Park, Fernando's Restaurant and the statue to the Goddess A-Ma.

Coloane Island is Macau's backyard and playground. It is about as large as peninsular Macau with a permanent population of only 2,500. The only population center is Coloane Village plus clusters of summer villas and resorts along the coastline. It offers beaches, wooded areas, eight nature trails and Macau's highest peak, on which the government has erected a 20-meter statue to the goddess A-Ma. The nature trails here and

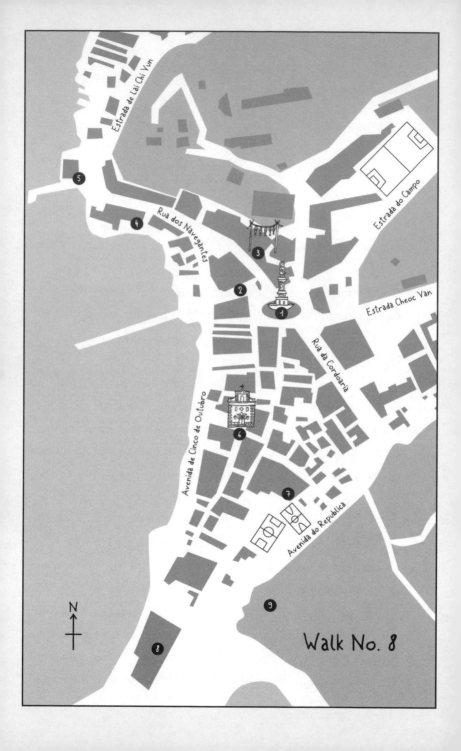

on Taipa are beyond the scope of this guide, although useful guides are offered by the Islands Municipal Council. The island's location close to the center of Macau's trade and its many coves and inlets made it a haven for pirates. Many residents of Coloane and nearby Taipa were happy to have Portugal extend its authority over the two islands in the mid-19th century. The Portuguese built a small artillery battery on the promontory behind the Tam Kung Temple in 1884. But pirates still infested the island as late as 1910, when the governor of the time, Eduardo Marques, decided to evict them. He landed troops on July 12 and was opposed by pirates who actually occupied the battery and turned its one cannon against them. Soon the pirates fled into the mountains. The "Battle of Coloane" is remembered in a stone obelisk in the front of the Chapel of St. Francis Xavier in Coloane Village. Gov. Marques later opened a barracks, stationed police and developed commerce. Today the island boasts a small boat-building industry and a modern container terminal on the isolated east coast.

Take bus 26 from the Lisboa Hotel to Coloane Village. It will drop you off at the town square, named rather pretentiously the **Largo Presidente Antonio Ramalho Eanes** (1), after a former president who served in Macau in the army. The square with its bronze statue to Cupid and pink concrete benches is worth lingering around. At one end is a pink Macanese building, once a police station, now a clinic. At another is the Alem Mar, a Cantonese seafood restaurant with some outdoor tables. Further along is **Lord Stow's Bakery** (2) which bills itself as the "creator of the egg tart now famous throughout Asia." Stow claimed to have introduced Portuguese egg tarts to Asia, which is credible considering that he franchised himself with outlets in Hong Kong, Tokyo, Taipei and Manila. They have become so popular with visitors that Stow had to open two other cafés in Coloane Village.

Just off the square on Rua das Gaivotas is the **Restaurante Espaco Lisboa** (3), a well-regarded family-operated establishment selling Portuguese and Macanese food in a charming village house. Nearby is the **Asian Artefacts** store on Rua dos Negociantes, which is a reliable source of restored Chinese furniture and other Asian handicrafts. Continuing along, one comes to the small but brightly painted **Sam Seng Temple** (4), one of four Chinese temples in Coloane. Painted a bright red, the small building manages to accommodate three deities: Kam Fa, Kun Iam and Wa Kong. It was built in 1865. The street turns into Rua dos Navegantes – the Street of Fishermen – which still has the flavor of the time when Coloane's fishing and salt-making businesses were at their height. It ends at the **Ponte Cais de Coloane** (5), the old ferry terminal that was the only link with Macau until the opening of the Taipa-Coloane Causeway in 1968. These days the only traffic comes from the slow procession of motorized sampans bringing fresh produce from China, which seems so close that you could practically wade across the water. Next to the pier is a humble little shop called in Portuguese the **Loja de Peixe Tong** that is Macau's best dried fish store, their pungent sea smell permeating the square. Climb up the hill past the marine police headquarters to the village of Lai Chi Van. Me Fai Gei restaurant is popular with workers from the village boatyard, although the yard itself no longer seems to bustle with much activity.

Backtrack to the square in front of the ferry terminal and then walk along the waterfront on Avenida Cinco de Outubro, lined with palm and banyan trees, which is often better known as the Coloane Praia (and the setting for some scenes of the Praia Grande from the television movie *Tai Pan*) – the only sounds, it seems, the low chug-chug of sampans in the bay and the clatter of mahjong tiles emanating from open doors. Soon one comes to the Largo Eduardo Marques with its monument to the victory over the pirates and wavy pavement of colored, black-and-white wavy tiles and an arcade containing the Nga Tim outdoor café with its somewhat eclectic menu.

At the far end stands the **Chapel of St. Francis Xavier** (6), an attractive, baroque little Catholic church with a gleaming cream-colored façade with white trim, five distinctive windows and a handsome little bell tower. It was built in 1928 and once contained a sacred relic, a bone from the right arm of St. Francis Xavier who died in  1552 on Sanchuan Island not far from Macau, and the remains of Christians persecuted in Japan. The bone was originally sent to Macau in 1618 from Goa and kept in St. Paul's church. After the fire that destroyed all but the church's façade, the bone was transferred to St. Joseph's Church. It was taken to Coloane in 1978. None of the relics are left, however. The bones of the martyrs were removed to a new crypt at St. Paul's on Macau and the bone of St. Francis was returned to the Chapel of St. Joseph's Seminary. The small Coloane church is still popular with Japanese Christians.

From the chapel one can either continue walking along the waterfront, past the attractive public library and the Luso-Chinese school (the only state-supported school in Macau, originally established for Portuguese-speaking children living on the island). One comes soon to the Tam Kung Temple Square. Or, one can walk through the attractive interior streets to the Travessa do Pagode and the **Kun Iam Temple** (7), built in 1862. It is distinguished by its oval moon gate window facing the water and gilded carved plaques. Sitting on the altar in the brightly decorated main hall is a wooden statue of Kun Iam, which survived a 1992 fire that otherwise gutted the building. Follow Loc Ian Lou to the end of the waterfront.

The space in front of the shrine is called **Tam Kung Temple Square** (8). It is a quiet, charming resting spot with two stone pavilions on either side of the temple, named "prosperity" and "affluence". A monument next to the temple, erected in 1826 by the Qing dynasty government, warns soldiers not to molest the fishermen. The temple itself was erected in 1862 after, it is said, fishermen saw a statue of Tam Kung, the Taoist protector of seafarers, floating in the water near the temple's present location. When the temple opened, the fishermen donated the bones of a whale, which were later used to make a model of a dragonboat that is used in processions and is one of the temple's most prized possessions. One more temple, the **Tin Hau Temple** (9) makes up Coloane Village's complement of shrines. It is the largest and oldest temple in the outlying islands, built in 1677 and extensively renovated since. The present complex comprises three main halls, all decorated with delicate and elegant wall paintings and figurines in the traditional style of South China folk art.

BEACHES AND PARKS

Coloane's several attractive beaches and parks are better reached by bus or taxi. However, one can hike from the village to **Cheoc Van Beach** (10), the southernmost point in Macau. Start by climbing the road behind the Tam Kung Temple around the promontory, along a wide trail and through a collection of villas, then down a stone staircase to the beach. By this time you have probably worked up a pretty strong appetite, which can be satisfied at the **Gondola Restaurant** (11) serving Italian food on a very pretty outdoor terrace. Also on the beach is the **Pousada de Coloane** (12). The pousada was the island's only hotel until the opening of the huge Westin Resort and golf course in 1992 further along the coast.

Macau's other beach, Hac Sa or 'black sand', is popular with locals, but most visitors come here only for one reason: Fernando's. It is undoubtedly the most famous Portuguese restaurant in

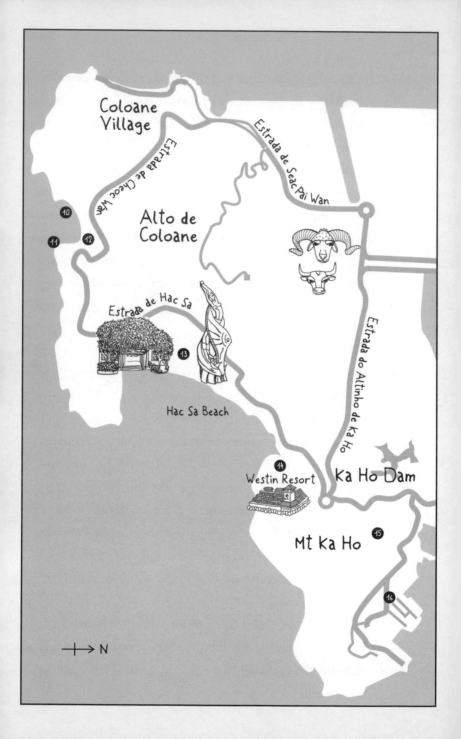

Macau. Considering its huge reputation, it is a little disconcerting to find out that **Restaurante Fernando** (13) looks not so much like a fancy European restaurant but an ordinary Chinese *dai pai dong*. It is organized in two parts, a small restaurant in the front and a somewhat larger establishment to the rear with an open-air bar area. One has to practically pass through the kitchen to get to the second dining area. Fernando's is down-home and unpretentious, which may be one secret to its enormous success. Red-checked tablecloths hang from clothes lines behind the building. Dogs sometimes poke their noses through the door. Sea breezes waft in through the windows. It is invariably packed with people. The food is good, ample and economical, but it has a kind of mass-produced quality. The standard salad has three ingredients: lettuce, tomatoes and onions. Chicken comes in three sizes but basically roasted on top of a pile of chips. It is tempting to look on Fernando's as a kind of high-class fast-food place.

EAST SIDE

The most attractive feature of Coloane's East Side is the seaside **Westin Macau Resort** (14), with a get-away-from-it-all ambiance. No casinos here, but plenty of other things to do. It is one of the few places in Macau designed for families. The **Kwan Hoi Heen** "restaurant with a view" is one of Macau's best Chinese restaurants. The cuisine is Cantonese. Try the tri-color (carrot, spinach, regular) steamed dumplings. They are served not in a traditional wooden bowl but on an exquisite ceramic plate.

The rest of the East Side offers little of interest unless one is determined to explore every corner of the enclave. **Ka Ho Village** (15) used to be a fairly important fishing town due to its location facing the Pearl River. But much of its importance died with the opening of the ferry to Coloane Village on the opposite side and, of course, the causeway to Taipa. Most of the villagers have migrated to other parts of Coloane or Macau proper. There are two small temples in the vicinity. One in the village is dedicated to Kun Iam. Another one is a small, dark and rather dank shrine right on the waterfront called the Sam Seng Temple. It boasts images of the three patron saints of Coloane. Also of interest on the east side is the **Church of Our Lady of Pain** (16), which used to serve as a sanctuary for the nearby leper colony. Its most arresting feature is a large iron crucifix at the peak designed by the Italian sculptor Francisco Messina of Milan.

Further Reading

Anyone interested in learning more about Macau's story is well advised to begin where I did, with Austin Coates' *Macao Narrative*. The former British civil servant in Hong Kong, and Macau aficionado, also wrote another useful history of Macau in the 19th century: *Macao and the British, Prelude to Hong Kong* (both Oxford University Press).

Another handy but slim volume of history is *Macau* by Cesar Guillen Nunez. It is published by the Oxford University Press as part of the *Images of Asia* series. Mr. Guillen Nunez, along with photographer Leong Ka Tai, is also the author of *Macao Streets*, a picture book that examines the life and history of peninsular Macau through its street names (also OUP).

For fuller accounts of Macau's history turn to *Encountering Macau* by Geoffrey C. Gunn (Westview Press, *op*). Another interesting take on Macau's history is provided by Jonathan Porter's *Macau: The Imaginary City* (Westview Press).

Father Manuel Teixeira has written numerous historical monographs about many aspects of Macau's history, although they are not easy to find in English. A few may be obtained through the government publications office. In writing this book I referred to his short history of the A-Ma Temple, *The Chinese Temple of Barra*.

Anyone interested in Macau's unique cuisine should look no farther than Annabel Jackson's *Macau on a Plate* (Roundhouse). She is also the author of a travel book, *Hong Kong, Macau and the Muddy Pearl* and is the co-author with Francisco M. Caldeira and photographer Leong Ka Tai of *Macau Gardens and Landscape Art* (Asia2000).

Fiction in English with a Macau setting is a rare treat. Still easily obtainable is Austin Coates' *City of Broken Promises*, which tells the story of the 18th-century benefactress Martha Merop (Oxford University Press). Martin Booth's *The Jade Pavilion* turns on the little-known fact that history's first airline hijacking occurred on a seaplane between Hong Kong and Macau (Atlantic Monthly Press, *op*).

Finally, anyone interested in Macau culture would delight in a colorful National Geographic-style periodical called *MacaU* published, if the vagaries of public financing have not intruded, by the Government Information Service. The tourist bureau also issues handy tourist and hiking guides in English to Taipa and Coloane available at the government tourist office in Taipa Village.

Getting There

Macau has an international airport, but most visitors arrive by way of Hong Kong. The jetfoils depart the Shun Tak Centre west of Central every 15 minutes during the day and at longer intervals in the evening and early morning. The trip takes about one hour. There are also direct ferry connections to Chek Lap Kok Airport.

Another ferry terminal is located on the Kowloon waterfront in Harbour City. The sailings are less frequent, usually one per hour on the hour, but the trip will cost about HK$100 less than from the Shun Tak Centre.

Old Macau hands seldom bother about the departure time printed on the ticket. They head straight for the standby line, which sounds better in Portuguese: the line of hope. Unless traffic is unusually heavy, say at the end of a long holiday weekend, you are almost certain to get a seat. However, you must arrive earlier, not later, than your confirmed departure time.

Ferries are currently sailing to a temporary pier on Taipa, near the airport, as well as to the main Ferry Terminal in Macau proper. Check the destination on your ticket. You can also fly to Macau on a helicopter from the Shun Tak Centre. It is considerably more expensive, but offers spectacular views of Hong Kong and Macau.

Useful websites

www.macautourism.gov.mo   www.macau-airport.com
www.turbojet.com.hk   www.nwff.com.hk
www.cotaijet.com.mo   www.skyshuttlehk.com

Macanese Cuisine

When the Portuguese arrived on this tiny blip on the coast of China, the only inhabitants were a few fishing families. More and more Chinese began to work in the enclave to support the Portuguese traders, but they remained a minority compared with the Portuguese, who arrived with their Asian wives and servants. In those days, the Chinese slipped back across the border at night to sleep in their homes in what we would call the mainland today.

It was the lack of an established culture in early Macau that allowed for a distinctive Macanese culture – and cooking – to develop. It is one of the world's great fusion cuisines, which entirely reflects the habits, experience and tastes of those who cooked and ate it, and continue to do so. The food has become a great signifier of the Macanese in Macau. To sample it is to understand Portugal's long experience in the East.

Today in Macau it is easy to sample not only Macanese and Portuguese cuisines but a myriad of other great cuisines such as Cantonese, Italian, French, Thai, in a host of world-class, even Michelin Guide-starred restaurants. Yet Macanese cuisine survives, even if it is relatively hard to find in the restaurant context. But what is Macanese cuisine?

It is perhaps simpler to define Macanese food by what it is not. There is some confusion over what could be called "Macau food," that is dishes for which Macau might be famous for but are not, strictly speaking, Macanese. Favorites such as roast pigeon, pork-chop buns, and even egg curry are eaten by locals and visitors alike, but they have grown up in the broader, multi-cuisine restaurant scene, not from within the Macanese domestic kitchen.

Macanese food is not just a simple cross between Portuguese and local Chinese. The Portuguese brought with them wives and servants from other parts of the then-vast Portuguese empire – Goa, Malacca, Timor and the East Indies. The cooking that emerged was, at its simplest, Portuguese dishes made with Portuguese techniques but with South China ingredients, accented with Southeast Asian herbs and spices.

Subsequently, many of the grander families embraced true Portuguese recipes made with all of the traditionally correct ingredients, and these should be regarded as Macanese too, particularly since several appear on traditional menus at weddings, baptisms and large parties. The less exalted families tended to incorporate more Cantonese-style dishes and ingredients, though there are, in fact, few totally Cantonese-inspired dishes in the Macanese lexicon. My book *Taste of Macau* (Hong Kong University Press) includes details of where to buy the essential ingredients to start experimenting with the cuisine at home.

Today, mainly the result of the Macanese diaspora, the cuisine is adapting itself to locally available ingredients across the world, often making substitutions, to produce dishes that have the spirit of Macanese cooking but are far from traditional. The use of fresh cod fish rather than salt cod *(bacalhau)* and the need to find an alternative for the almost-extinct fish sauce *balichao* are good examples of the evolution. But then no cuisine ever stands still.

Following are some of the restaurants that serve the best or most typical Macanese dishes.

- **Carlos**, Rua Cidade de Braga, NAPE. This is a restaurant with plenty of atmosphere, very popular with local residents who seem to eat there every day. Ask Carlos what is the special of the day.
- **Restaurante Litoral**, 261A Rua do Almirante Sergio. Try the minced meat with soy sauce and *porco balichao*, pork with shrimp paste and tamarind. It has a branch restaurant near Taipa Village.
- **Riquexo** (Rickshaw), 69 Avenida do Sidonio Pais. Don't be turned off by its appearance as a high-school cafeteria. The Macanese food here is considered as good as it gets.
- **APOMAC**, Avenida do Sidonio Pais, 49B Edificio China Plaza. A club for retired Macanese, the restaurant is open to the public and serves a great range of home-made Macanese dishes.

– Annabel Jackson

Glossary

You may find the following list of Portuguese and Chinese terms helpful in exploring Macau. Note that the Chinese names for Avenida Almeida Ribeiro and St. Paul's are useful for getting around in a taxi.

Avenida	Avenue
Balichao	Shrimp paste
Beco	Lane or alley
Calçada	A steep street
Canidrome	Dog racing stadium
Cozinha	Kitchen
Dai Sam Ba	Cantonese for St. Paul's
Esplanada	Waterfront path
Estrada	Street or path
Feng shui	Chinese geomancy
Galinha a Portuguesa	Portuguese chicken
Gao	Bay
Istmo	Isthmus
Jardim	Garden
Kun Iam	Chinese goddess of mercy
Largo	Plaza or square
Leal	Loyal
Ma Kok Miu	Chinese for A-Ma Temple
Macanese	Macau people of mixed blood
Macao	Alternate (American) spelling

NAPE	Acronym for a reclaimed area
Nata	Popular cream pastry
Ou-Mun	Cantonese for Macau
Pataca	Macau currency
Patua	Macau dialect
Portas do Cerco	Barrier Gate
Pousada	Portuguese inn
Praia	Waterfront
Rua	Street or road
San Ma Lo	Chinese name for Avenida Almeida Ribeiro, Macau's main street
SAR	Special Administrative Region
Travessa	Alley
Zhuhai	Chinese border city opposite Macau

ABOUT THE AUTHOR

For 14 years Todd Crowell worked as Senior Writer for *Asiaweek*, the English-language news magazine published in Hong Kong by Time Warner. In addition to *Explore Macau* he has published two other books: *Farewell, My Colony: Last Years in the Life of British Hong Kong* (1998) and *Tokyo: City on the Edge* (2001). He has contributed regularly to the *Christian Science Monitor* and *Asian Wall Street Journal* among other publications and has worked as an editor and writer in Hong Kong, Thailand and now Japan, where he serves as Japan correspondent for *Asia Sentinel*. He keeps a blog at asiacable.blogspot.com.

ACKNOWLEDGEMENTS

I would like to extend my thanks to all those who helped me explore Macau's byways. They include Annabel Jackson, oracle on all things pertaining to Macau's unique cuisine and a contributor to this book. I'd also like to thank Harald Bruning, probably the best informed journalist on Macau, and finally Teresa Gomes and her colleagues at the Macau Government Tourist Office for their invaluable assistance.

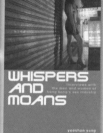